Stack-n-Pack

Grades 3-5

Connecting Mathematical Representations

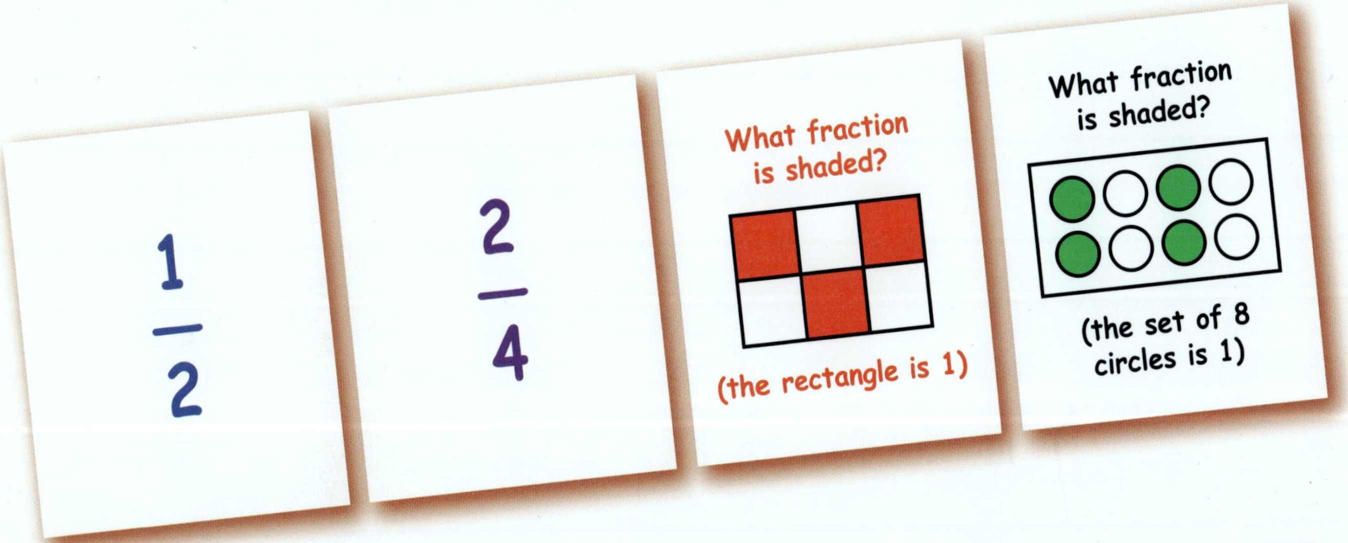

1
—
2

2
—
4

What fraction is shaded?

(the rectangle is 1)

What fraction is shaded?

(the set of 8 circles is 1)

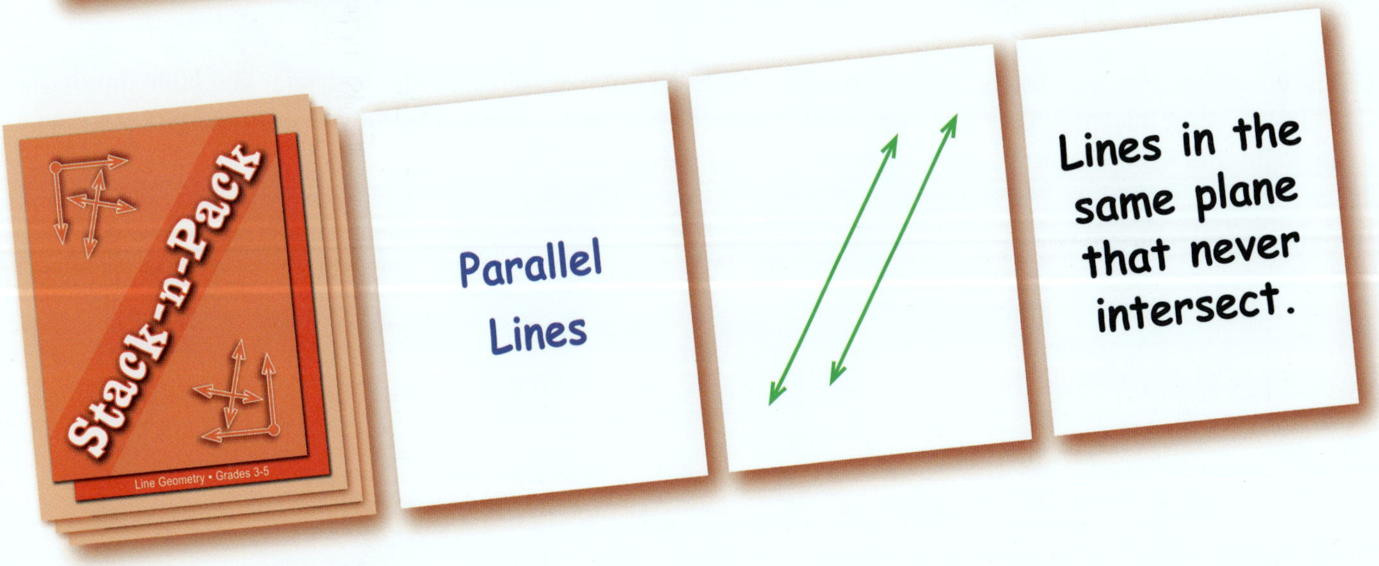

Stack-n-Pack

Line Geometry • Grades 3-5

Parallel Lines

Lines in the same plane that never intersect.

Dr. Janie Cates & Dr. Jill Reddish

Published by Learning Advantage.

Printed in the United States of America.

Order Number 6074
ISBN-10: 0-927726-17-3
ISBN-13: 978-0-927726-17-7

10 09 08 07 06 05 04 03

P.O. Box 368
Timnath, CO 80547
www.learningadvantage.com

Contact us toll free 866-564-8251 or info@learningadvantage.com
to become a retail dealer or to locate a dealer near you!

Stack-n-Pack

Grades 3-5

Table of Contents

Stack-n-Pack Information Chart

	Stack-n-Pack	Stack Starter	# of Cards in Completed Stack	Cards in the Completed Stack
1.	Place Value Identification	Place Value Name (ones, tens, ...)	4	**Place Value Name,** 3 Numbers with Place Value underlined
2.	Multiplication Facts	Product (30, 42, ...)	4	**Product,** 3 sets of factors for the product
3.	2-D and 3-D Geometric Shapes	Shape Name (circle, cube, ...)	3	**Shape Name,** 2 Pictures of the shape
4.	Polygon Classification	Polygon Name (square, rhombus, ...)	4	**Polygon Name,** Picture of Polygon, Side Definition, Angle Definition
5.	LCM and GCF	Set of Numbers (4 and 5; 3, 6 and 8; ...)	3	**Set of 2 or 3 numbers,** GCF, LCM
6.	Equivalent Fractions	Simplified Fraction ($\frac{1}{2}$, $\frac{1}{4}$, ...)	4	**Simplified Fraction,** Equivalent Fraction in Fraction form, as part of a rectangle, as part of a set
7.	Addition & Multiplication Properties	Property Name (identity, commutative, ...)	4	**Property Name,** variable representation, 2 examples
8.	Line Geometry	Geometric Term (ray, line, ...)	4	**Name,** Definition, 2 Pictorial Representations
9.	Area and Perimeter	Shape (there are 2 of each shape)	4	**Shape,** Formulas, Area, Perimeter/Circumference
10.	Algebraic Reasoning	Variable with Answer (x = 3)	3	**Variable,** 2 Equations that have the same value as the variable

Note: The Stack Starter for the Grades 3-5 games is in blue.

Directions for Playing "Stack-n-Pack"

1. Form groups of 3-4 players.

2. Each player is dealt 4 cards. The remaining cards are placed face down in the center of the table. This is the draw pile. There is no discard pile.

3. Play begins with the person to the left of the dealer and continues clockwise around the table.

4. The first player can start a stack with the appropriate stack starter card (see Stack-n-Pack Information Chart). This is NOT his/her stack. Any player can play on any stack. Once a stack has been started, the other cards in the stack may be played in any order. After playing his/her card, the first player draws a card from the draw pile ending his/her turn. If the first player does not have a stack starter, then he/she must PASS.

5. The next player has the option of playing on any stack laid on the table or beginning a new stack. Only ONE (1) card can be played at each turn. After playing his/her card, the player draws a card from the draw pile ending his/her turn.

6. Play continues in this manner with each player either playing on a stack or beginning a new one. Players must play if they are able. Otherwise, they must pass and lose their turn. Players must also remember to draw after they play their card.

7. A completed stack contains the total number of cards and representations described in the Stack-n-Pack Information Chart. The number of cards and representations necessary to complete a stack varies with each game. The player who completes the stack by playing the final card wins that stack.

8. Once all the cards have been drawn, play continues until no more cards can be played.

9. The game is over when the last stack has been completed. The player with the most stacks is the winner.

Notes about Stack-n-Pack Games

- Students practice recognizing various representations of mathematical topics by completing stacks of 3, 4, or 5 cards, depending on the topic.
- The object of the game is to capture the most "stacks." A stack must be started with the stack starter card (described in the Stack-n-Pack Information Chart).
- The played cards are laid face-up on the table and anyone can play on any stack. After the stack starter card is played, the remaining representations may be played in any order.
- The player who completes the "stack" by playing the last representation wins that "stack."
- Players may use a WILD card to capture a "stack," but may not start a "stack" with a WILD card.

Note about the WILD cards: If you use the wild cards in a stack, then there will be 2 cards that will not be used during the game. A player may also choose to use his turn to exchange a played wild card for one that is in his/her hand and will play on the stack. If this is done, then the player makes the play and does not draw from the deck. The next player then takes his/her turn and play continues as usual.

Game Variation for 1 or 2 Players

This game can be used as a matching game in which students can play individually or with a partner. To do this, you might want to only use 2 of the representations. As students are successful with 2 of the representations, you can make it more challenging by including the others.

Stack-n-Pack Extensions

To extend and refine students' understanding of mathematical representations, it is important to engage students in reflecting and writing about their experiences. The following journal prompts may be useful in helping students think about what they have learned from the Stack-n-Pack games.

1. After playing this game, I now better understand...
2. After playing this game, I still have questions about...
3. After playing this game, I want to be sure that I remember...
4. When trying to figure out how stacks go together, I think about...
5. I learned something new about math today. I learned...
6. The most challenging part of playing Stack-n-Pack is...
7. When I got stuck in the game, I...
8. What strategies did you use to play Stack-n-Pack?
9. How did what you learned from the Stack-n-Pack game reinforce or clarify what you already knew about the concept?
10. Draw pictures to represent an additional stack for this game. Be sure to include all the cards for a complete stack. Explain why your stack is appropriate for the game.

Where's the Math?

The importance of using multiple representations in mathematics should be emphasized throughout students' mathematical education. Stack-n-Pack is designed to help students better understand mathematical representations, including pictorial, written, and symbolic. Through playing Stack-n-Pack students can begin to recognize and make connections among various mathematical representations. This enables students to think more flexibly about mathematics.

The National Council of Teachers of Mathematics (NCTM) strongly supports students having access to mathematical representations. According to NCTM (2000) "representations should be treated as essential elements in supporting students' understanding of mathematical concepts and relationships" (p. 67). Being able to make connections within mathematics helps students become better problem solvers. "When students can connect mathematical ideas, their understanding is deeper and more lasting" (NCTM, p. 64). Making connections between representations helps students understand how representations can be used to model mathematical ideas and relationships. Stack-n-Pack is a tool to help students begin to make connections between various mathematical representations.

Correlation to the Standards

Correlation to NCTM's *Principles and Standards for School Mathematics*
Stack-n-Pack for Grades 3-5

	Numbers and Operations	Algebra	Geometry	Measurement	Data Analysis and Probability	Problem Solving	Reasoning and Proof*	Communication*	Connections	Representation
Place Value Identification	×					×	×	×	×	×
Multiplication Facts	×					×	×	×	×	×
2-D and 3-D Geometric Shapes			×			×	×	×	×	×
Polygon Classification			×			×	×	×	×	×
GCF and LCM	×					×	×	×	×	×
Equivalent Fractions	×					×	×	×	×	×
Addition and Multiplication Properties	×	×				×	×	×	×	×
Line Geometry			×			×	×	×	×	×
Area and Perimeter				×		×	×	×	×	×
Algebraic Reasoning		×				×	×	×	×	×

* The Reasoning and Proof and Communication standards are incorporated in the Stack-n-Pack Extensions.

Place Value Identification

Stack-n-Pack	Stack Starter	# of Cards in Completed Stack	Cards in the Completed Stack
Place Value Identification	Place Value Name (ones, tens, ...)	4	Place Value Name, 3 Numbers with Place Value Underlined

Note: The Stack Starter is in blue.

Directions for Playing "Stack-n-Pack"

1. Form groups of 3-4 players.
2. Each player is dealt 4 cards. The remaining cards are placed face down in the center of the table. This is the draw pile. There is no discard pile.
3. Play begins with the person to the left of the dealer and continues clockwise around the table.
4. The first player can start a stack with the appropriate stack starter card (see Stack-n-Pack Information Chart above). This is NOT his/her stack. Any player can play on any stack. Once a stack has been started, the other cards in the stack may be played in any order. After playing his/her card, the first player draws a card from the draw pile ending his/her turn. If the first player does not have a stack starter, then he/she must PASS.

(Directions continued on back)

5. The next player has the option of playing on any stack laid on the table or beginning a new stack. Only ONE (1) card can be played at each turn. After playing his/her card, the player draws a card from the draw pile ending his/her turn.

6. Play continues in this manner with each player either playing on a stack or beginning a new one. Players must play if they are able. Otherwise, they must pass and lose their turn. Players must also remember to draw after they play their card.

7. A completed stack contains the total number of cards and representations described in the Stack-n-Pack Information Chart. The number of cards and representations necessary to complete a stack varies with each game. The player who completes the stack by playing the final card wins that stack.

8. Once all the cards have been drawn, play continues until no more cards can be played.

9. The game is over when the last stack has been completed. The player with the most stacks is the winner.

ones	tens	hundreds	thousands
ten thousands	hundred thousands	millions	tenths

Stack-n-Pack
75.8
749
Place Value Identification ▪ Grades 3-5

$36\underline{2}$	hundredths
$42\underline{1}.23$	thousandths
$5\underline{3}9$	ten-thousandths
$1,3\underline{5}2$	$13,45\underline{6}$

Stack-n-Pack
75.8
749
Place Value Identification ▪ Grades 3-5

3,002	1,289.251
115,341	749
289,333	23,899
68,219.3	15,632.4

Stack-n-Pack
75.8
749
Place Value Identification ▪ Grades 3-5
Stack-n-Pack
75.8
749
Place Value Identification ▪ Grades 3-5
Stack-n-Pack
75.8
749
Place Value Identification ▪ Grades 3-5
Stack-n-Pack
75.8
749
Place Value Identification ▪ Grades 3-5
Stack-n-Pack
75.8
749
Place Value Identification ▪ Grades 3-5
Stack-n-Pack
75.8
749
Place Value Identification ▪ Grades 3-5
Stack-n-Pack
75.8
749
Place Value Identification ▪ Grades 3-5
Stack-n-Pack
75.8
749
Place Value Identification ▪ Grades 3-5

1,346,890

389,214

45,689,123

127,451

16,234,589

290,571.23

9,123,490.1

500,000

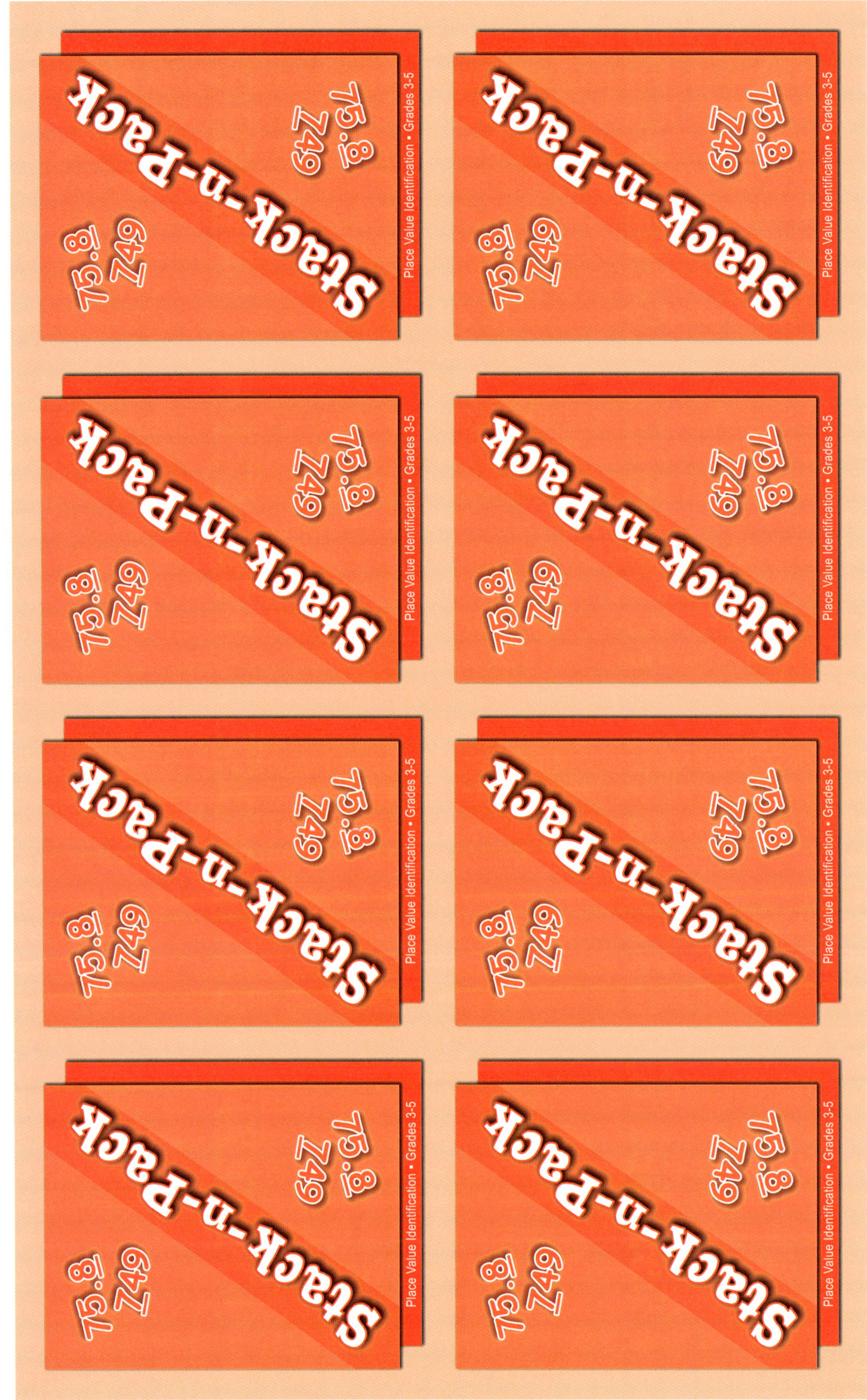
Stack-n-Pack
75.8
749
Place Value Identification ▪ Grades 3-5

75.8	5,321.234	438.94	1,257.341
732.509	0.561	2.6511	148.932

Stack-n-Pack
75.8
749
Place Value Identification ▪ Grades 3-5

Place Value Wild Card hundreds tens tenths ones	0.29721
Place Value Wild Card hundreds tens tenths ones	61.2981
	0.97341
	267.2130

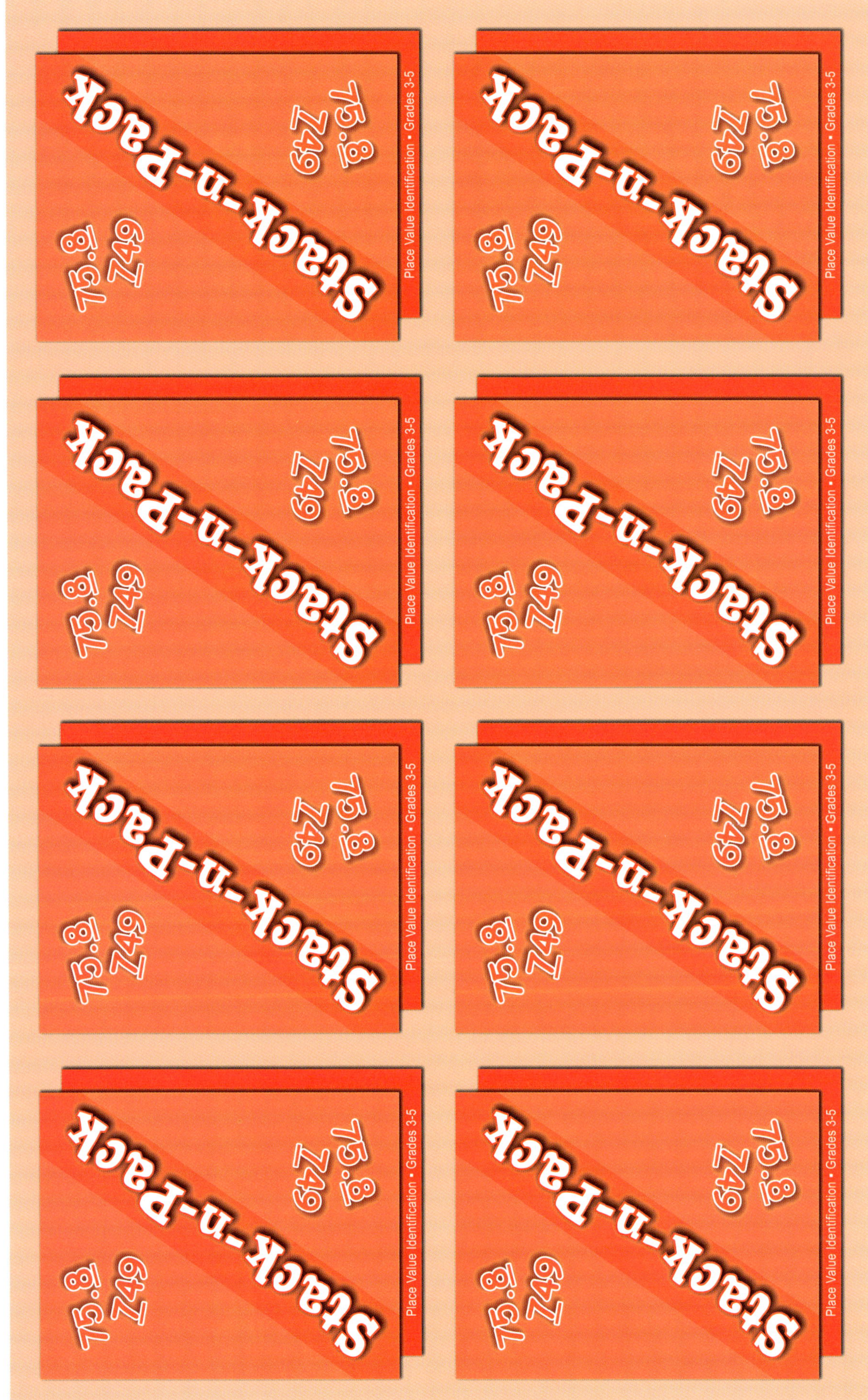
Stack-n-Pack
75.8
749
Place Value Identification • Grades 3-5

Multiplication Facts

Stack-n-Pack	Stack Starter	# of Cards in Completed Stack	Cards in the Completed Stack
Multiplication Facts	Product (30, 42, ...)	4	Product, 3 Sets of Factors for the Product

Note: The Stack Starter is in blue.

Directions for Playing "Stack-n-Pack"

1. Form groups of 3-4 players.
2. Each player is dealt 4 cards. The remaining cards are placed face down in the center of the table. This is the draw pile. There is no discard pile.
3. Play begins with the person to the left of the dealer and continues clockwise around the table.
4. The first player can start a stack with the appropriate stack starter card (see Stack-n-Pack Information Chart above). This is NOT his/her stack. Any player can play on any stack. Once a stack has been started, the other cards in the stack may be played in any order. After playing his/her card, the first player draws a card from the draw pile ending his/her turn. If the first player does not have a stack starter, then he/she must PASS.

(Directions continued on back)

5. The next player has the option of playing on any stack laid on the table or beginning a new stack. Only ONE (1) card can be played at each turn. After playing his/her card, the player draws a card from the draw pile ending his/her turn.

6. Play continues in this manner with each player either playing on a stack or beginning a new one. Players must play if they are able. Otherwise, they must pass and lose their turn. Players must also remember to draw after they play their card.

7. A completed stack contains the total number of cards and representations described in the Stack-n-Pack Information Chart. The number of cards and representations necessary to complete a stack varies with each game. The player who completes the stack by playing the final card wins that stack.

8. Once all the cards have been drawn, play continues until no more cards can be played.

9. The game is over when the last stack has been completed. The player with the most stacks is the winner.

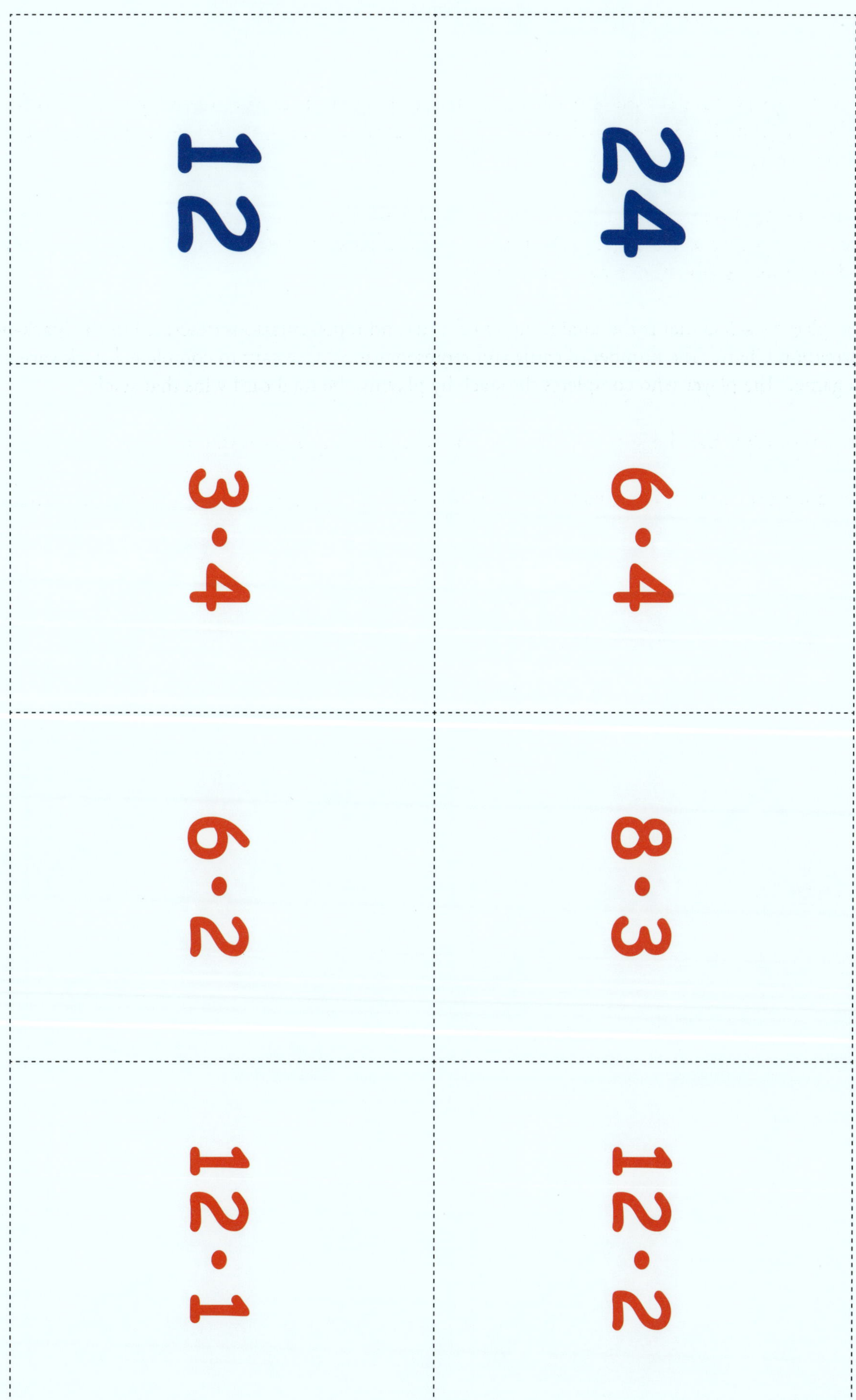
12
24
3·4
6·4
6·2
8·3
12·1
12·2

Stack-n-Pack
3·6
9·2
Multiplication Facts ▪ Grades 3-5
Stack-n-Pack
3·6
9·2
Multiplication Facts ▪ Grades 3-5
Stack-n-Pack
3·6
9·2
Multiplication Facts ▪ Grades 3-5
Stack-n-Pack
3·6
9·2
Multiplication Facts ▪ Grades 3-5
Stack-n-Pack
3·6
9·2
Multiplication Facts ▪ Grades 3-5
Stack-n-Pack
3·6
9·2
Multiplication Facts ▪ Grades 3-5
Stack-n-Pack
3·6
9·2
Multiplication Facts ▪ Grades 3-5
Stack-n-Pack
3·6
9·2
Multiplication Facts ▪ Grades 3-5

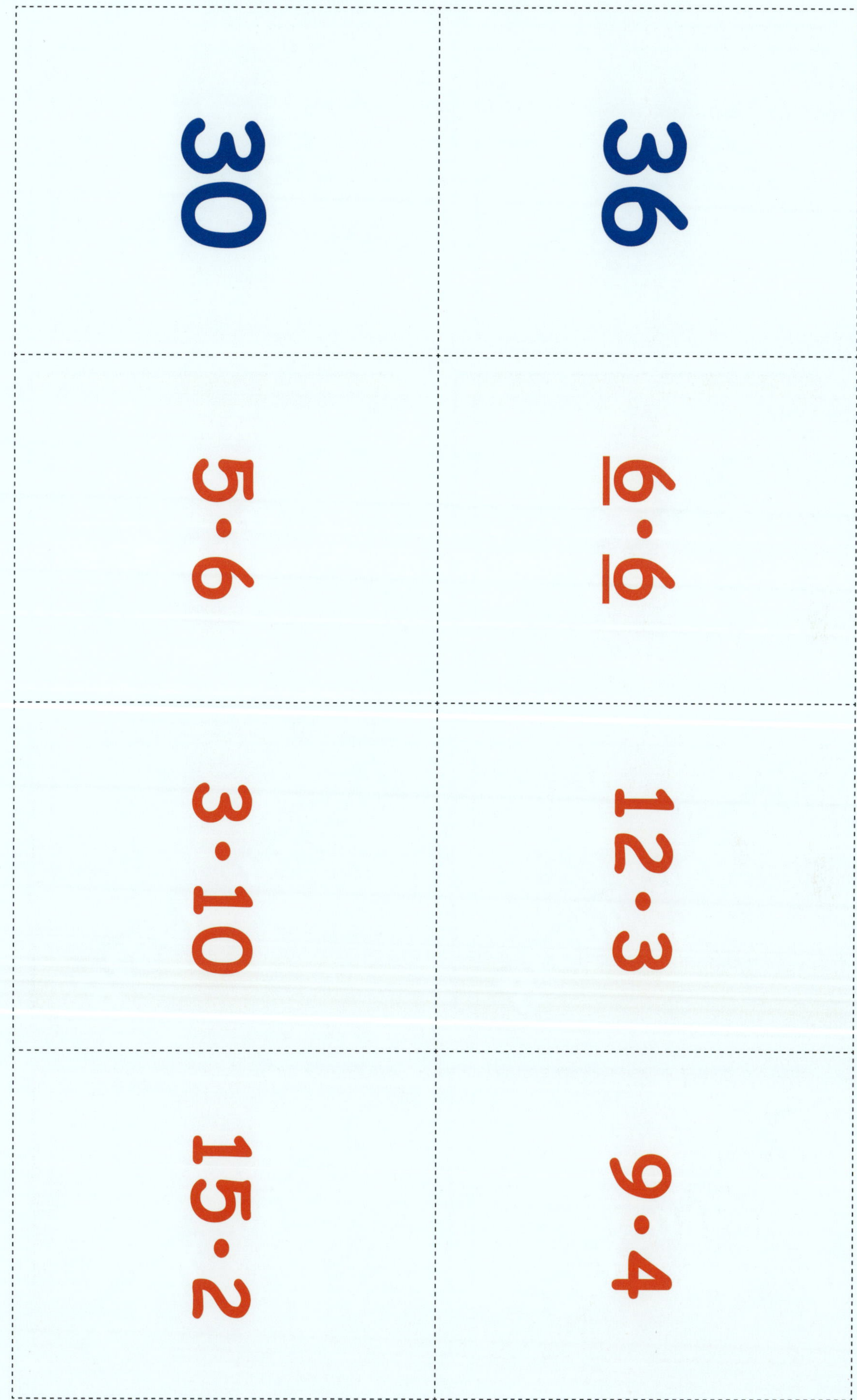
30
36
5·6
6·6
3·10
12·3
15·2
9·4

Stack-n-Pack
Multiplication Facts ▪ Grades 3-5

18
3·6
9·2
6·3
48
6·8
4·12
24·2

Stack-n-Pack
3·6
Multiplication Facts ▪ Grades 3-5

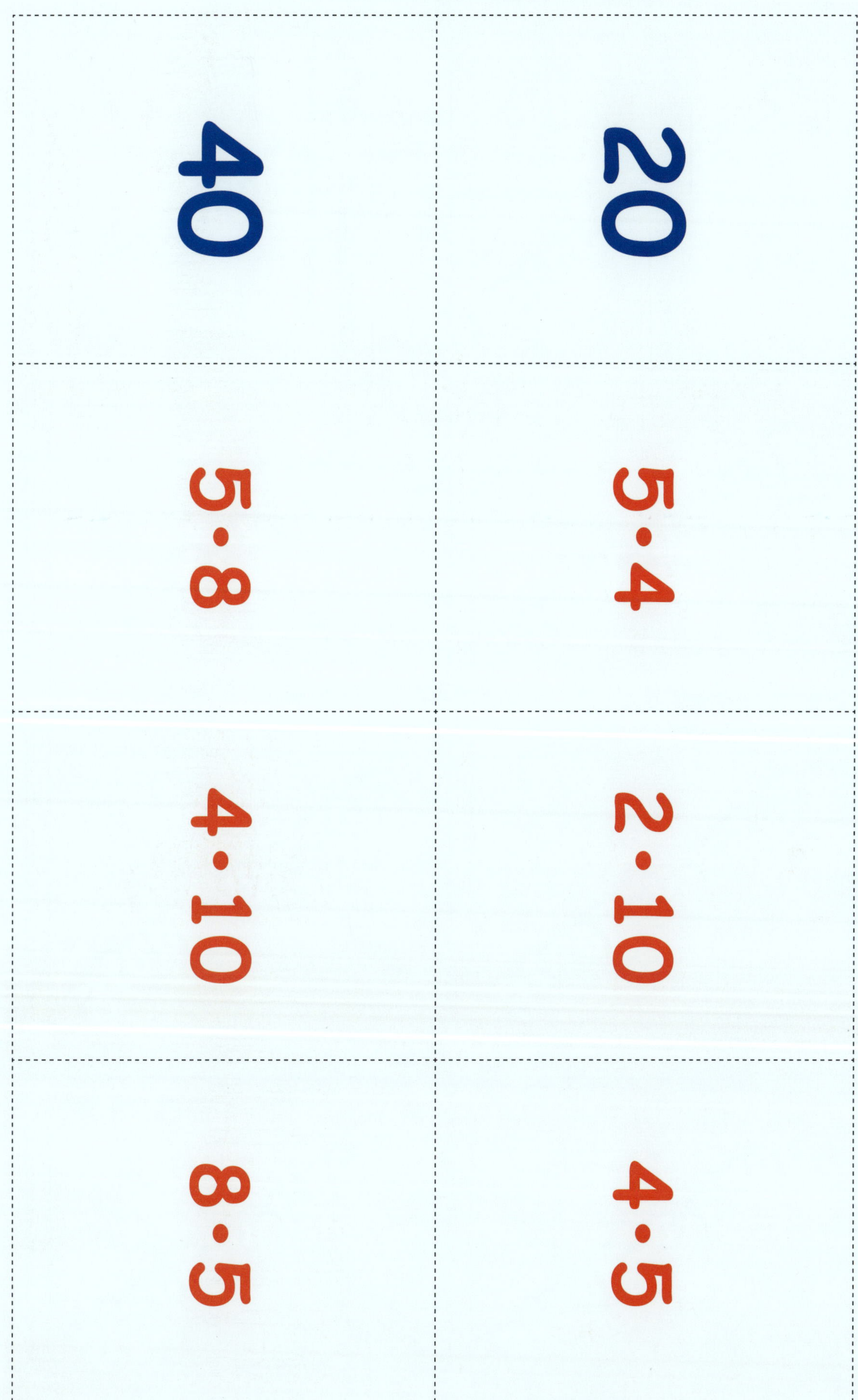
40
20
5 • 8
5 • 4
4 • 10
2 • 10
8 • 5
4 • 5

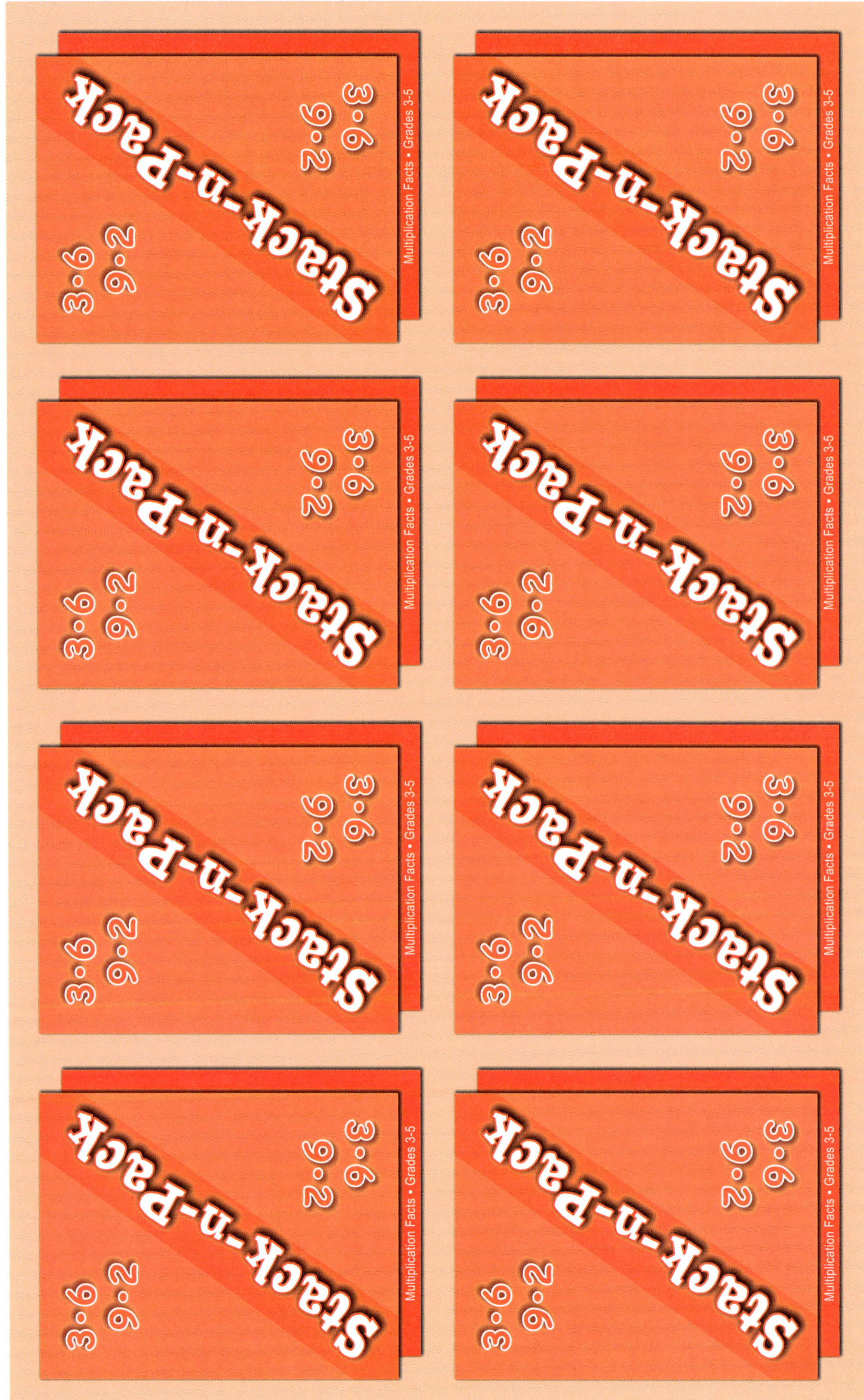
Stack-n-Pack
3·6
9·2
Multiplication Facts ▪ Grades 3-5

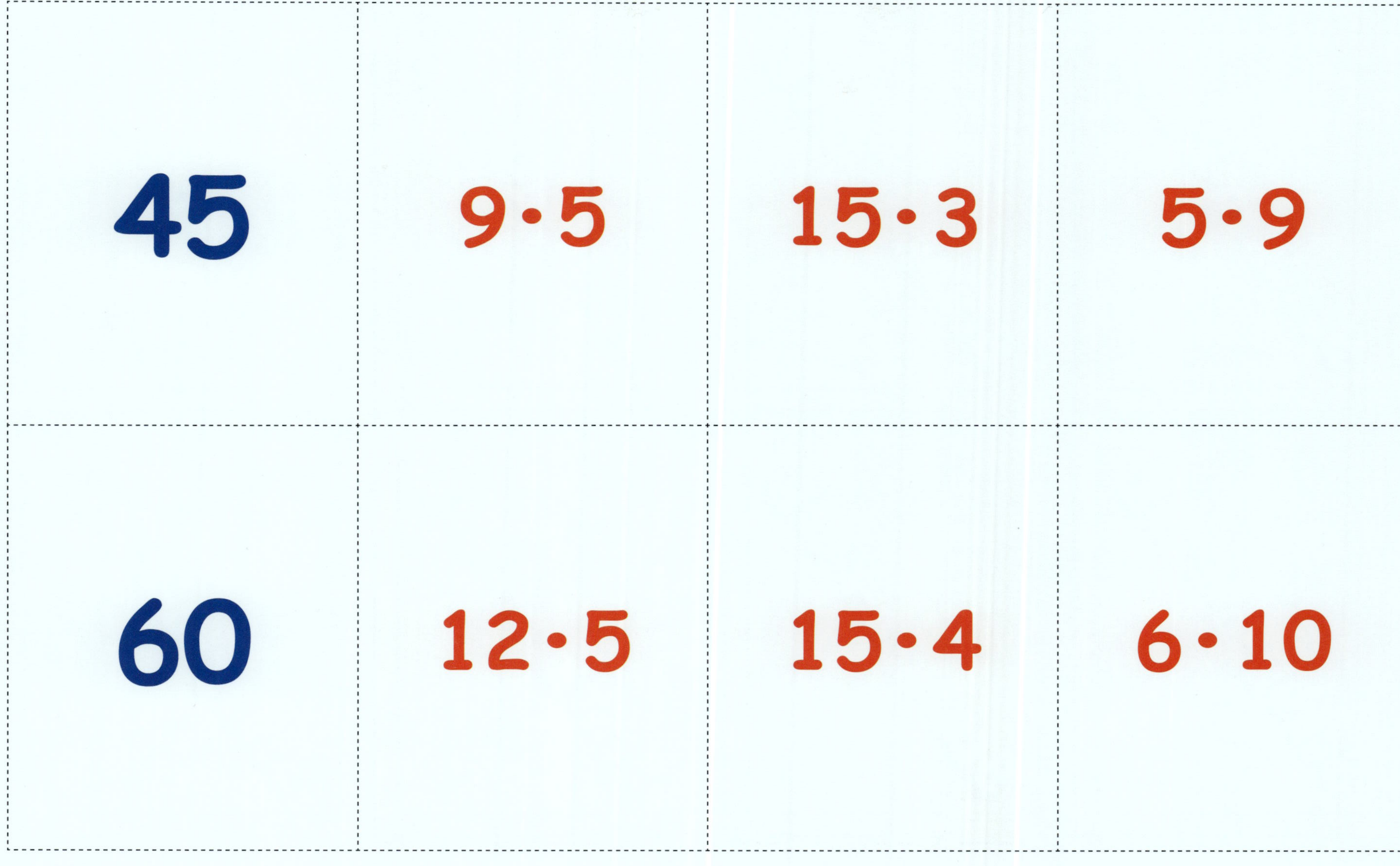
45
9·5
15·3
5·9
60
12·5
15·4
6·10

Stack-n-Pack
3·6
9·2
Multiplication Facts ▪ Grades 3-5

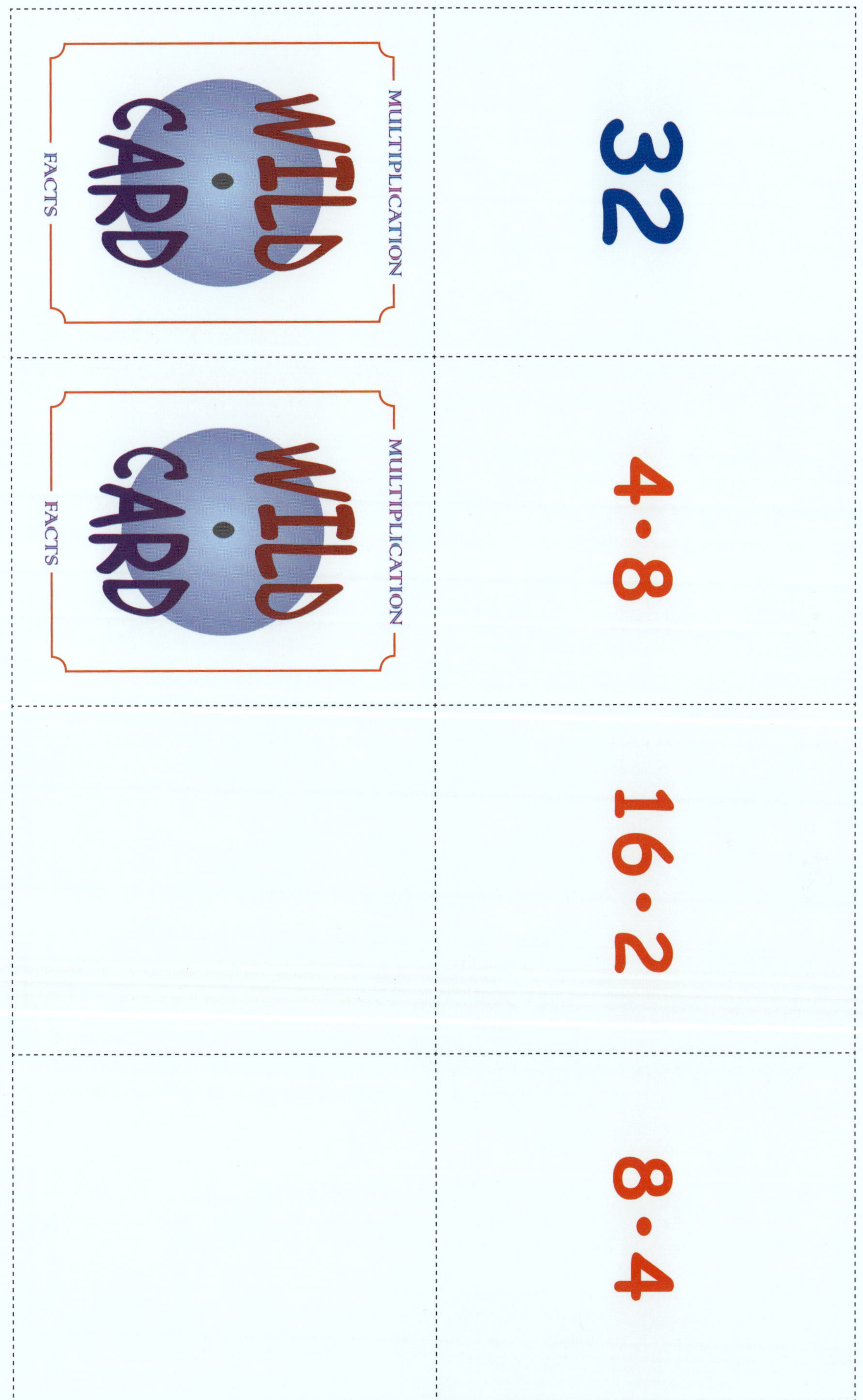
MULTIPLICATION
WILD CARD
FACTS
32
MULTIPLICATION
WILD CARD
FACTS
4 · 8
16 · 2
8 · 4

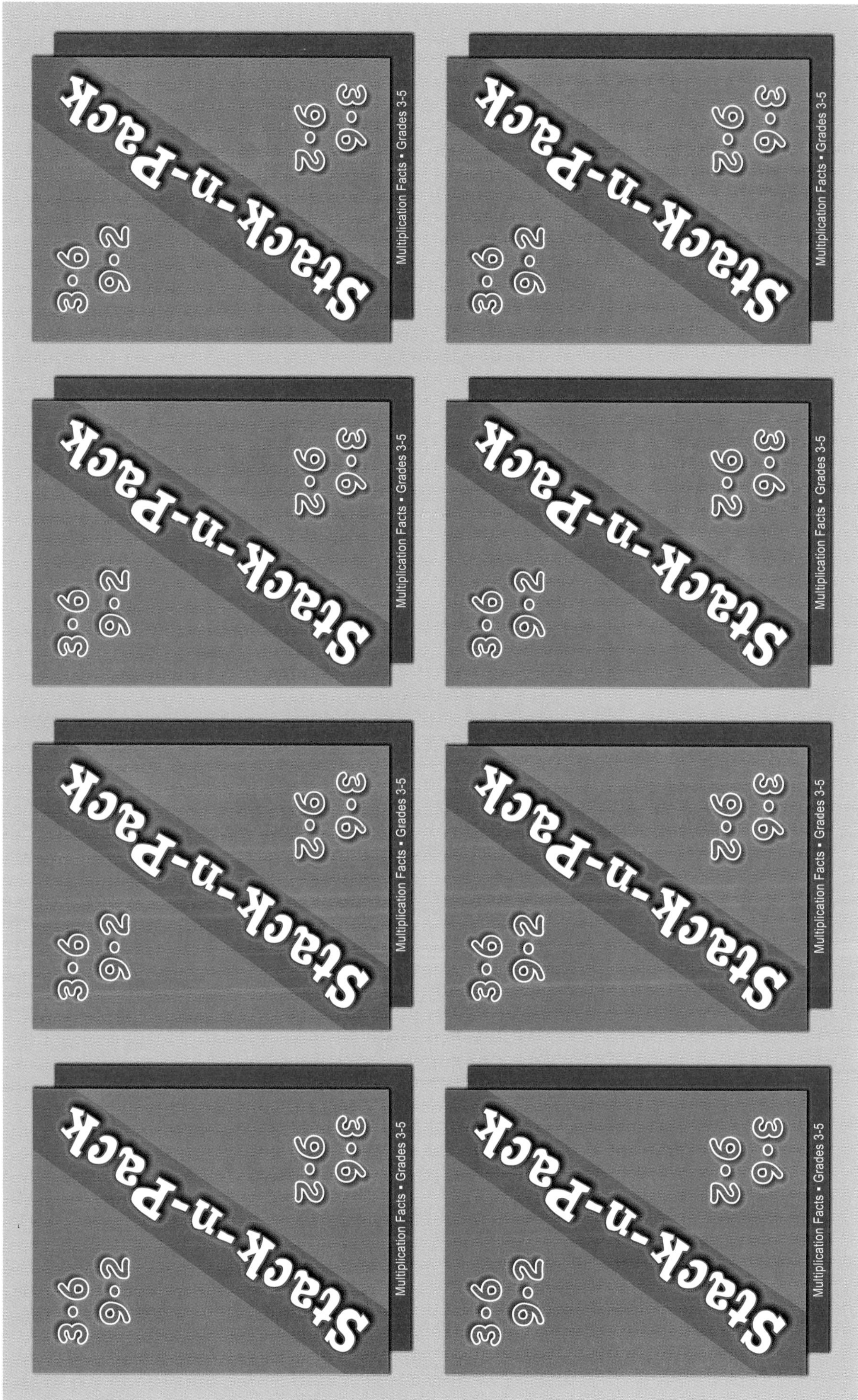
Stack-n-Pack
3·6
9·2
Multiplication Facts ▪ Grades 3-5

2-D and 3-D Geometric Shapes

Stack-n-Pack	Stack Starter	# of Cards in Completed Stack	Cards in the Completed Stack
2-D and 3-D Geometric Shapes	Shape Name (circle, cube, ...)	3	Shape Name, 2 Pictures of the Shape

Note: The Stack Starter is in blue.

Directions for Playing "Stack-n-Pack"

1. Form groups of 3-4 players.
2. Each player is dealt 4 cards. The remaining cards are placed face down in the center of the table. This is the draw pile. There is no discard pile.
3. Play begins with the person to the left of the dealer and continues clockwise around the table.
4. The first player can start a stack with the appropriate stack starter card (see Stack-n-Pack Information Chart above). This is NOT his/her stack. Any player can play on any stack. Once a stack has been started, the other cards in the stack may be played in any order. After playing his/her card, the first player draws a card from the draw pile ending his/her turn. If the first player does not have a stack starter, then he/she must PASS.

(Directions continued on back)

5. The next player has the option of playing on any stack laid on the table or beginning a new stack. Only ONE (1) card can be played at each turn. After playing his/her card, the player draws a card from the draw pile ending his/her turn.

6. Play continues in this manner with each player either playing on a stack or beginning a new one. Players must play if they are able. Otherwise, they must pass and lose their turn. Players must also remember to draw after they play their card.

7. A completed stack contains the total number of cards and representations described in the Stack-n-Pack Information Chart. The number of cards and representations necessary to complete a stack varies with each game. The player who completes the stack by playing the final card wins that stack.

8. Once all the cards have been drawn, play continues until no more cards can be played.

9. The game is over when the last stack has been completed. The player with the most stacks is the winner.

Rhombus	Rectangle (but, it is not a square)
Ellipse	Circle
Pentagon	Triangle
Hexagon	Square

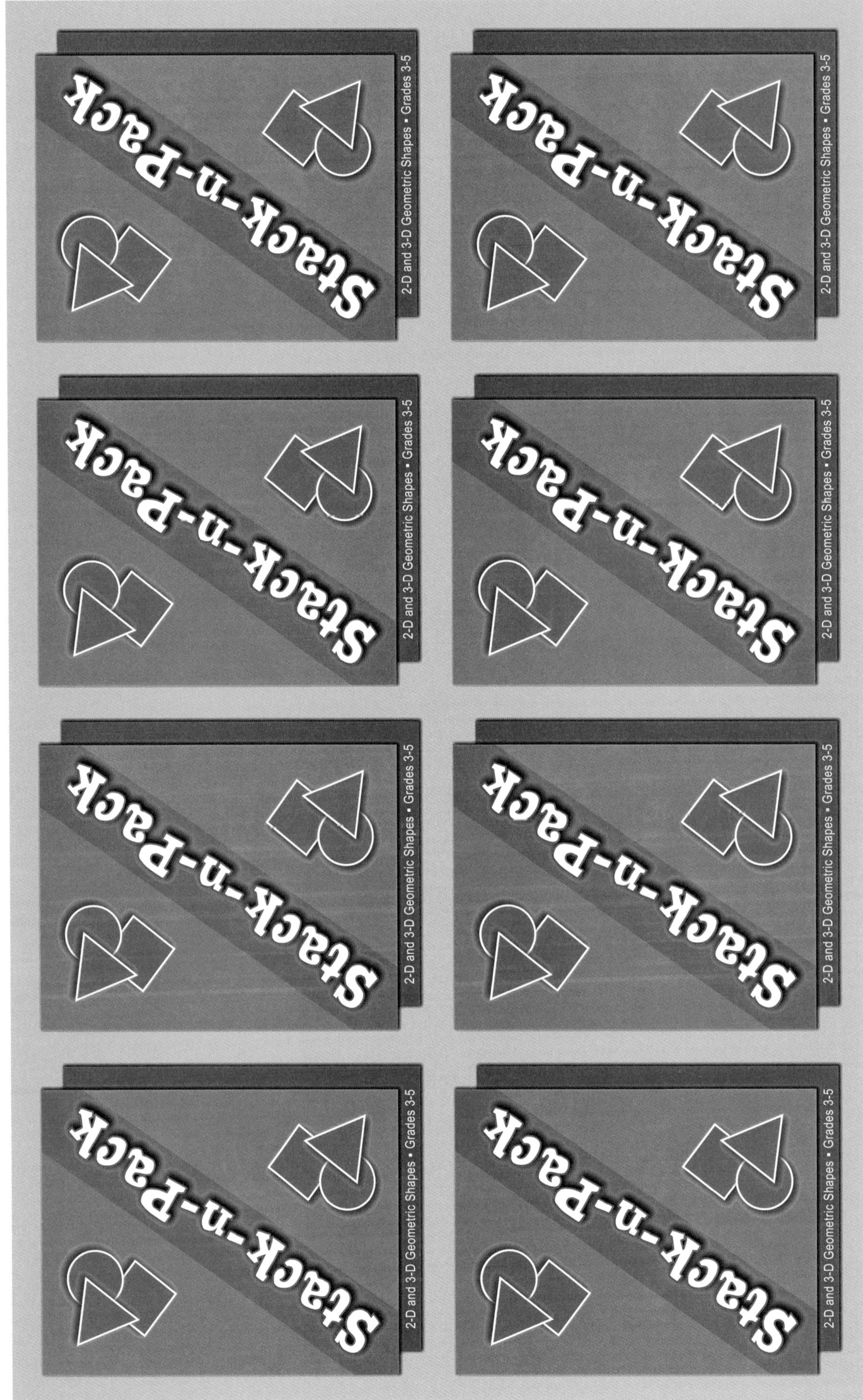
Stack-n-Pack
2-D and 3-D Geometric Shapes ▪ Grades 3-5
Stack-n-Pack
2-D and 3-D Geometric Shapes ▪ Grades 3-5
Stack-n-Pack
2-D and 3-D Geometric Shapes ▪ Grades 3-5
Stack-n-Pack
2-D and 3-D Geometric Shapes ▪ Grades 3-5
Stack-n-Pack
2-D and 3-D Geometric Shapes ▪ Grades 3-5
Stack-n-Pack
2-D and 3-D Geometric Shapes ▪ Grades 3-5
Stack-n-Pack
2-D and 3-D Geometric Shapes ▪ Grades 3-5
Stack-n-Pack
2-D and 3-D Geometric Shapes ▪ Grades 3-5

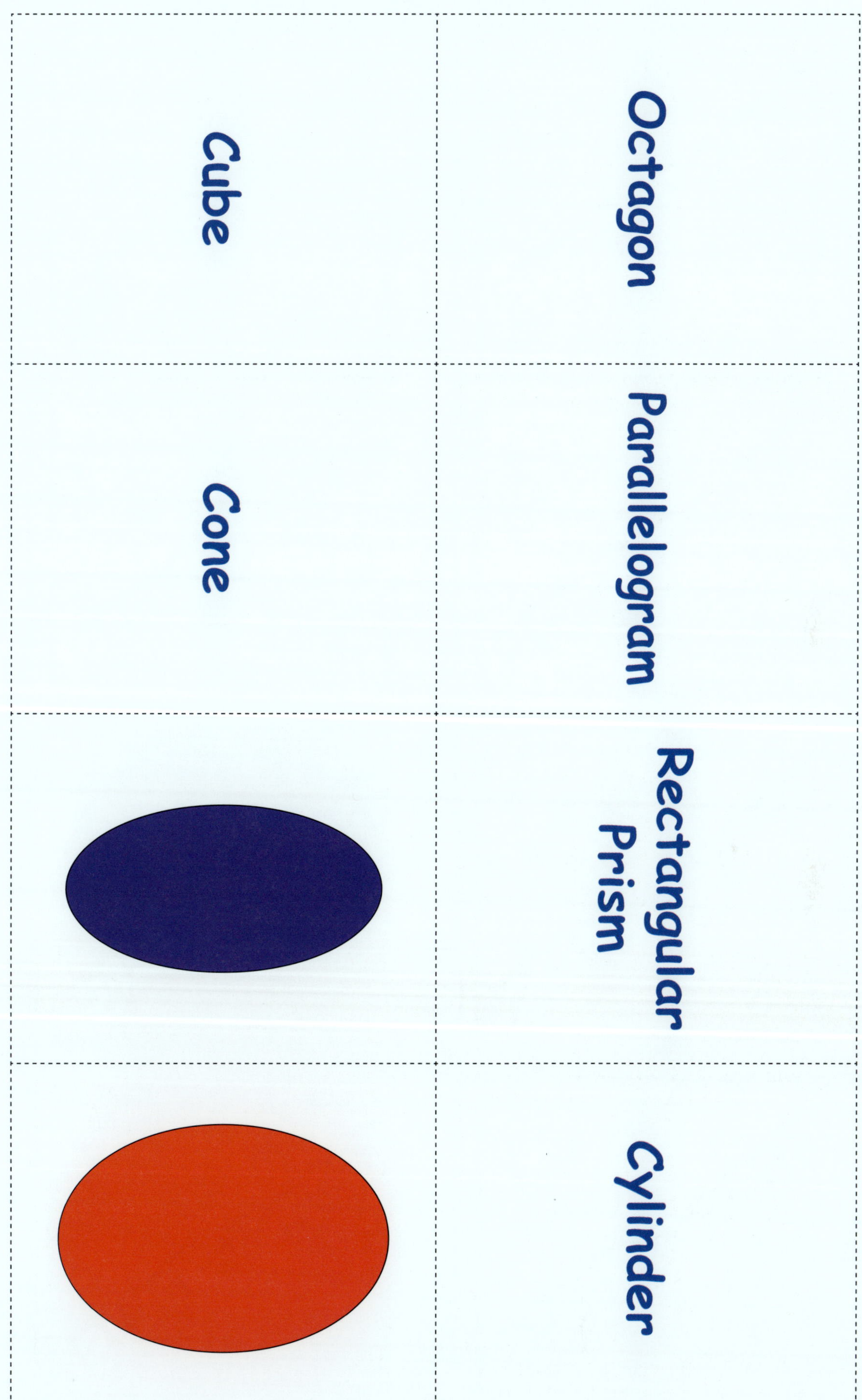
Cube
Octagon
Cone
Parallelogram
Rectangular Prism
Cylinder

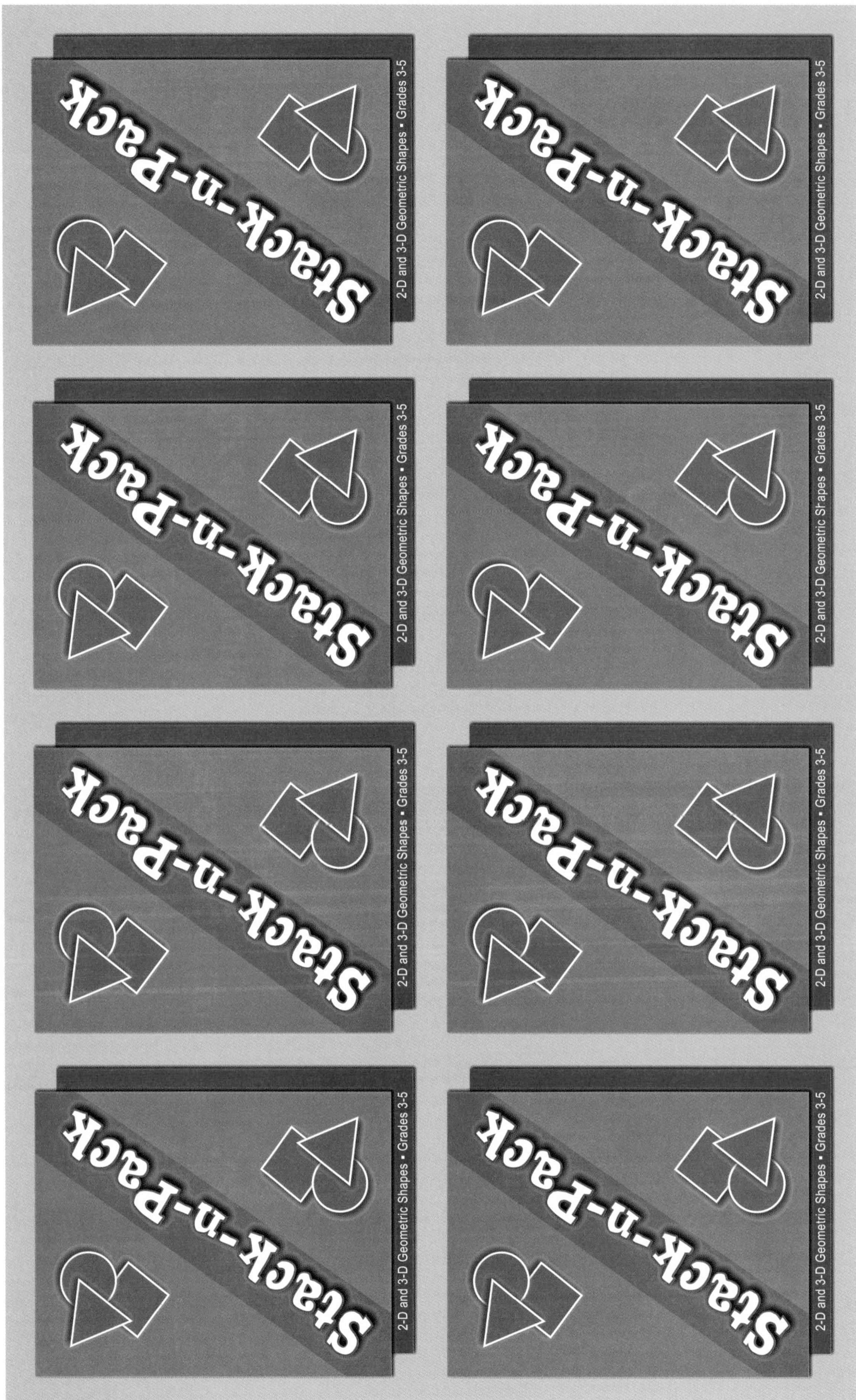
Stack-n-Pack
2-D and 3-D Geometric Shapes ▪ Grades 3-5
Stack-n-Pack
2-D and 3-D Geometric Shapes ▪ Grades 3-5
Stack-n-Pack
2-D and 3-D Geometric Shapes ▪ Grades 3-5
Stack-n-Pack
2-D and 3-D Geometric Shapes ▪ Grades 3-5
Stack-n-Pack
2-D and 3-D Geometric Shapes ▪ Grades 3-5
Stack-n-Pack
2-D and 3-D Geometric Shapes ▪ Grades 3-5
Stack-n-Pack
2-D and 3-D Geometric Shapes ▪ Grades 3-5
Stack-n-Pack
2-D and 3-D Geometric Shapes ▪ Grades 3-5

Stack-n-Pack
2-D and 3-D Geometric Shapes ▪ Grades 3-5

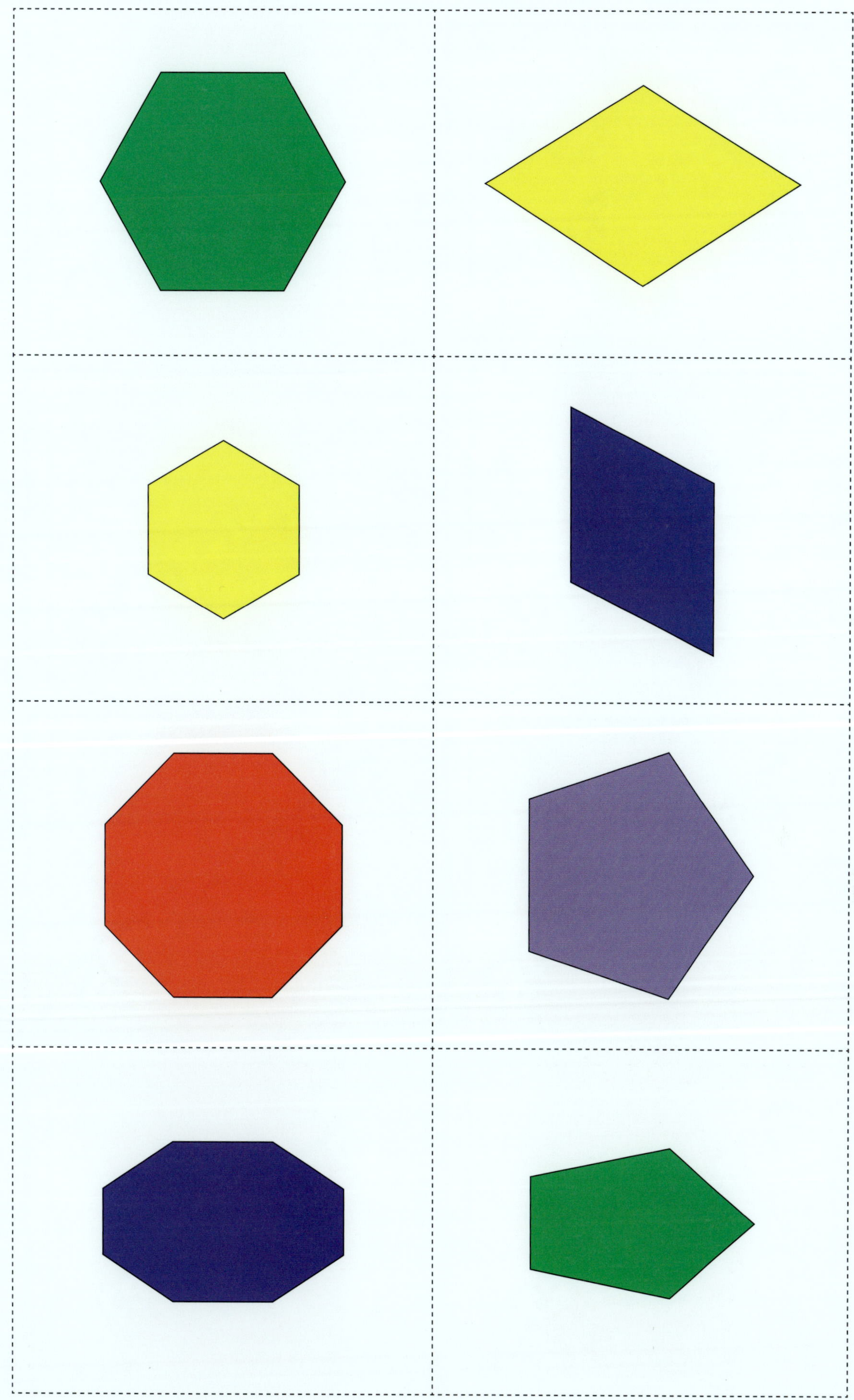

Stack-n-Pack
2-D and 3-D Geometric Shapes ▪ Grades 3-5
Stack-n-Pack
2-D and 3-D Geometric Shapes ▪ Grades 3-5
Stack-n-Pack
2-D and 3-D Geometric Shapes ▪ Grades 3-5
Stack-n-Pack
2-D and 3-D Geometric Shapes ▪ Grades 3-5
Stack-n-Pack
2-D and 3-D Geometric Shapes ▪ Grades 3-5
Stack-n-Pack
2-D and 3-D Geometric Shapes ▪ Grades 3-5
Stack-n-Pack
2-D and 3-D Geometric Shapes ▪ Grades 3-5
Stack-n-Pack
2-D and 3-D Geometric Shapes ▪ Grades 3-5

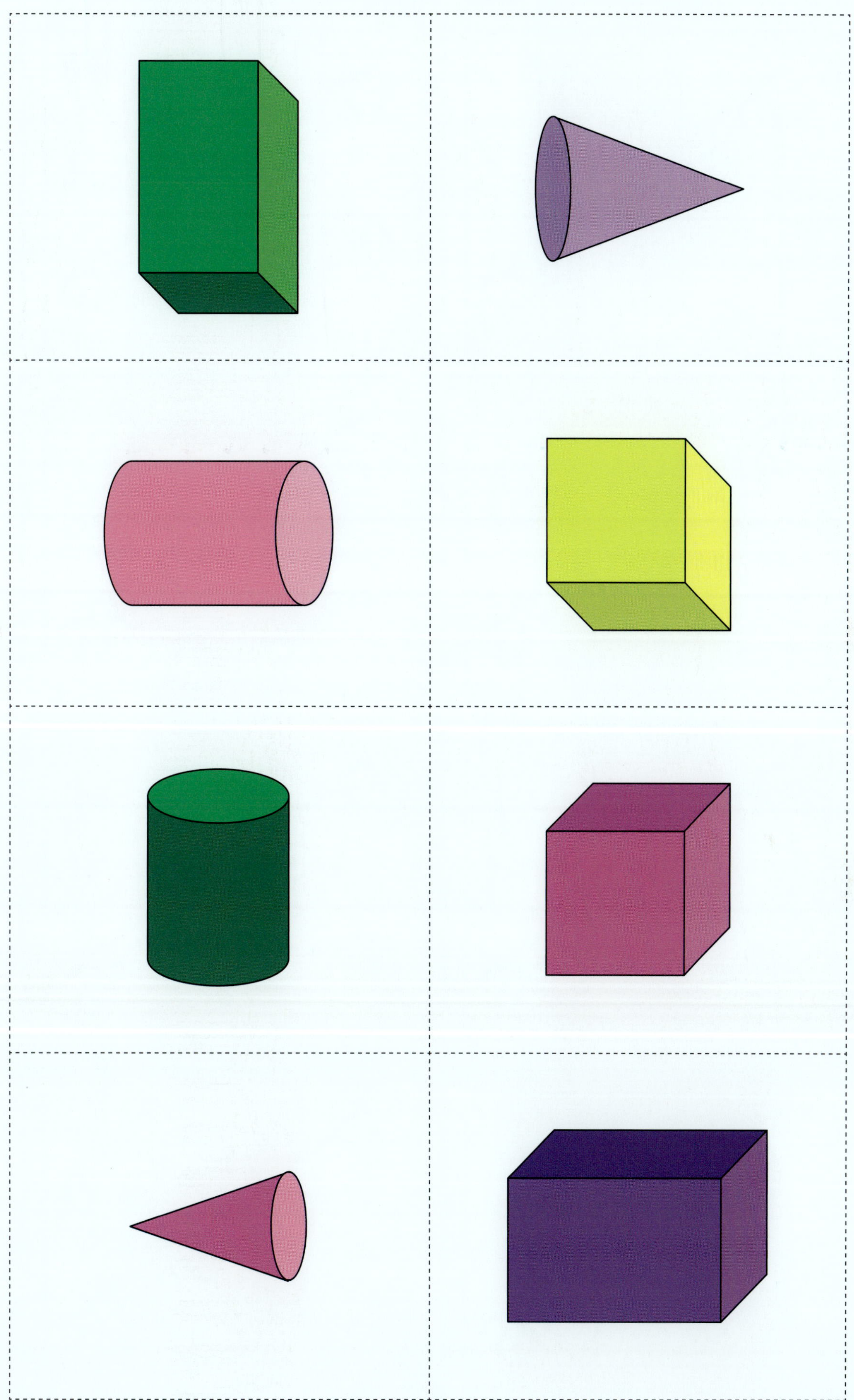

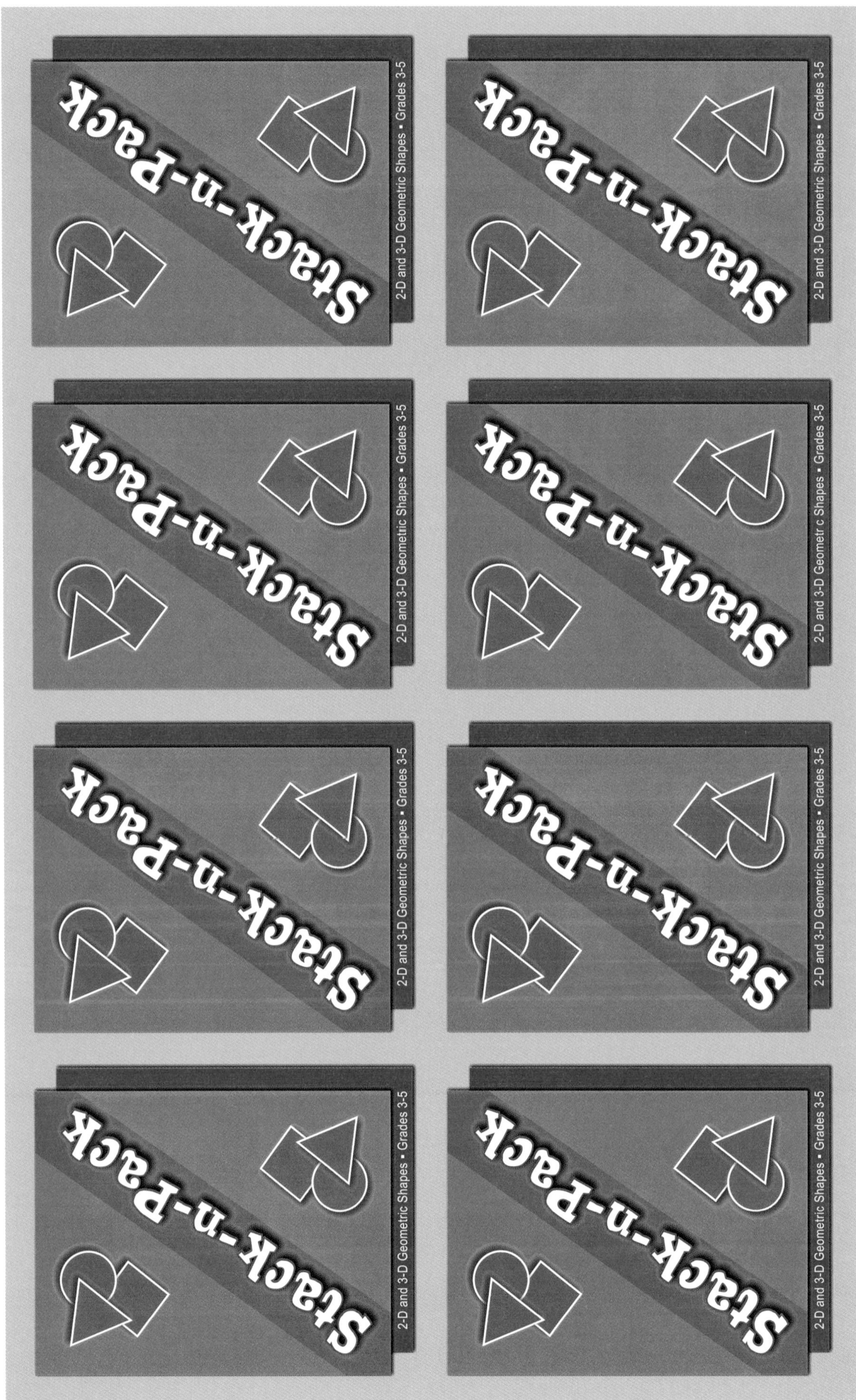
Stack-n-Pack
2-D and 3-D Geometric Shapes ▪ Grades 3-5

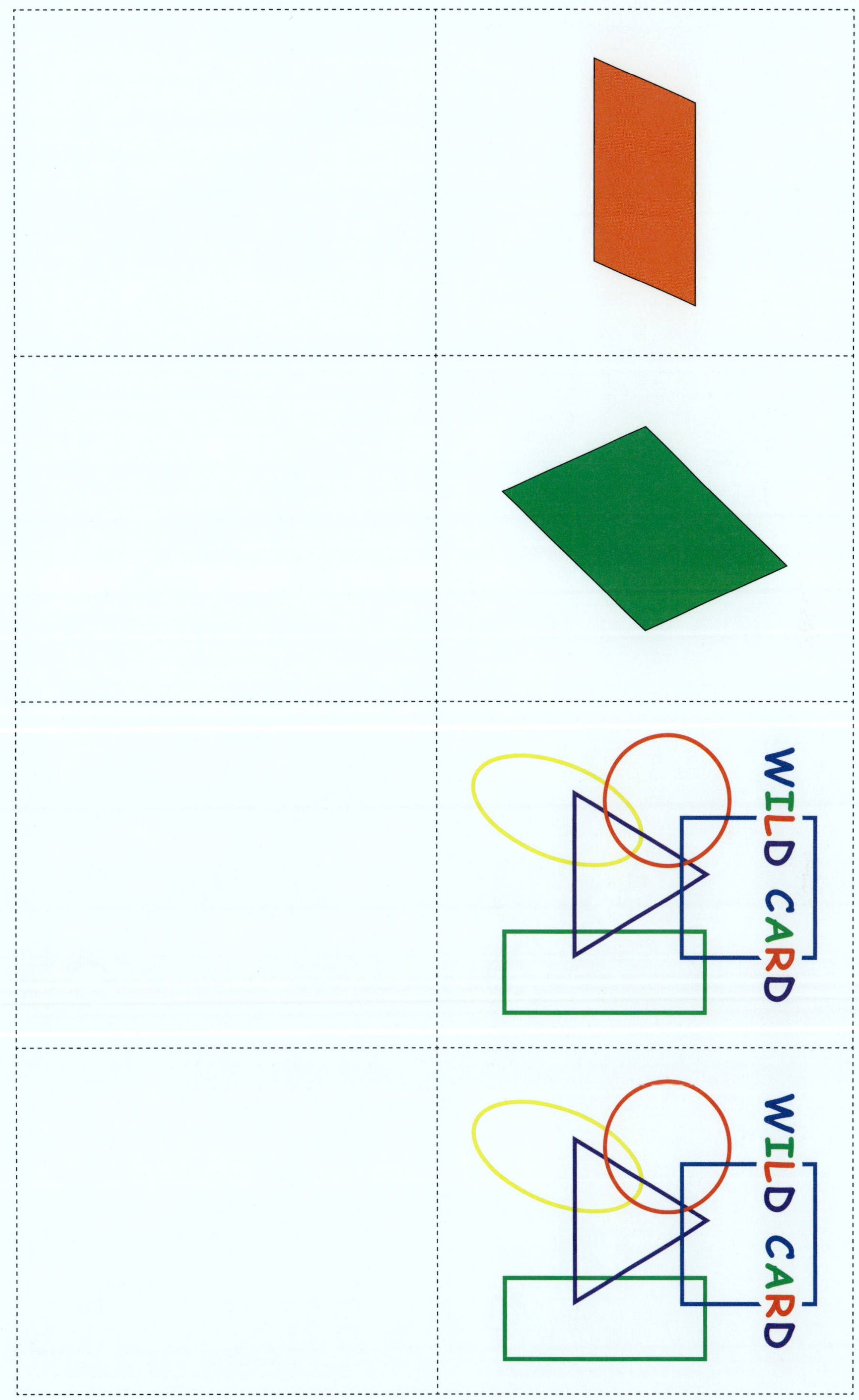
WILD CARD
WILD CARD

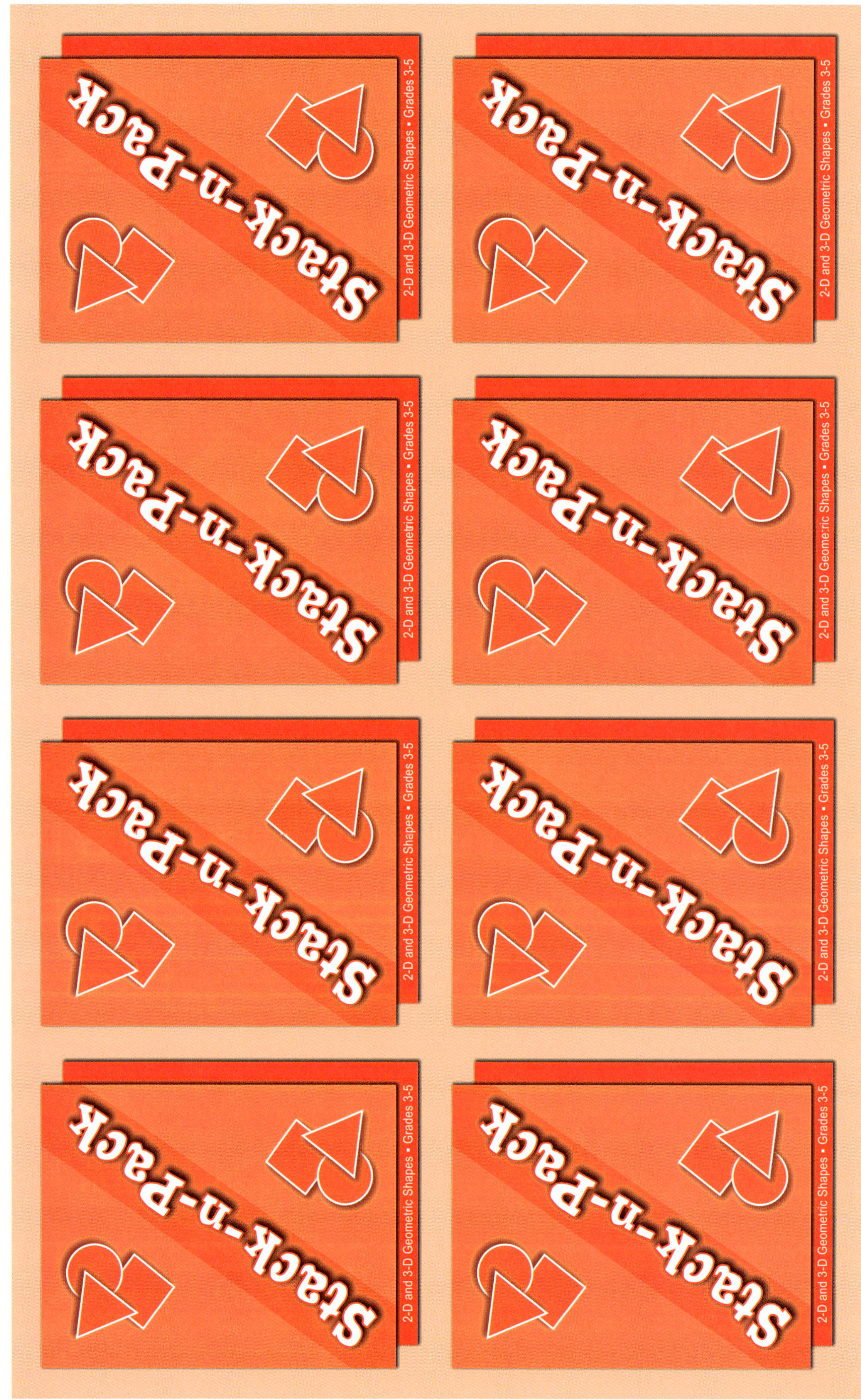
Stack-n-Pack
2-D and 3-D Geometric Shapes • Grades 3-5
Stack-n-Pack
2-D and 3-D Geometric Shapes • Grades 3-5
Stack-n-Pack
2-D and 3-D Geometric Shapes • Grades 3-5
Stack-n-Pack
2-D and 3-D Geometric Shapes • Grades 3-5
Stack-n-Pack
2-D and 3-D Geometric Shapes • Grades 3-5
Stack-n-Pack
2-D and 3-D Geometric Shapes • Grades 3-5
Stack-n-Pack
2-D and 3-D Geometric Shapes • Grades 3-5
Stack-n-Pack
2-D and 3-D Geometric Shapes • Grades 3-5

Polygon Classification

Stack-n-Pack	Stack Starter	# of Cards in Completed Stack	Cards in the Completed Stack
Polygon Classification	Polgon Name (square, rhombus, ...)	4	Polygon Name, Picture of Polygon, Side Definition, Angle Definition

Note: The Stack Starter is in blue.

Directions for Playing "Stack-n-Pack"

1. Form groups of 3-4 players.
2. Each player is dealt 4 cards. The remaining cards are placed face down in the center of the table. This is the draw pile. There is no discard pile.
3. Play begins with the person to the left of the dealer and continues clockwise around the table.
4. The first player can start a stack with the appropriate stack starter card (see Stack-n-Pack Information Chart above). This is NOT his/her stack. Any player can play on any stack. Once a stack has been started, the other cards in the stack may be played in any order. After playing his/her card, the first player draws a card from the draw pile ending his/her turn. If the first player does not have a stack starter, then he/she must PASS.

(Directions continued on back)

5. The next player has the option of playing on any stack laid on the table or beginning a new stack. Only ONE (1) card can be played at each turn. After playing his/her card, the player draws a card from the draw pile ending his/her turn.

6. Play continues in this manner with each player either playing on a stack or beginning a new one. Players must play if they are able. Otherwise, they must pass and lose their turn. Players must also remember to draw after they play their card.

7. A completed stack contains the total number of cards and representations described in the Stack-n-Pack Information Chart. The number of cards and representations necessary to complete a stack varies with each game. The player who completes the stack by playing the final card wins that stack.

8. Once all the cards have been drawn, play continues until no more cards can be played.

9. The game is over when the last stack has been completed. The player with the most stacks is the winner.

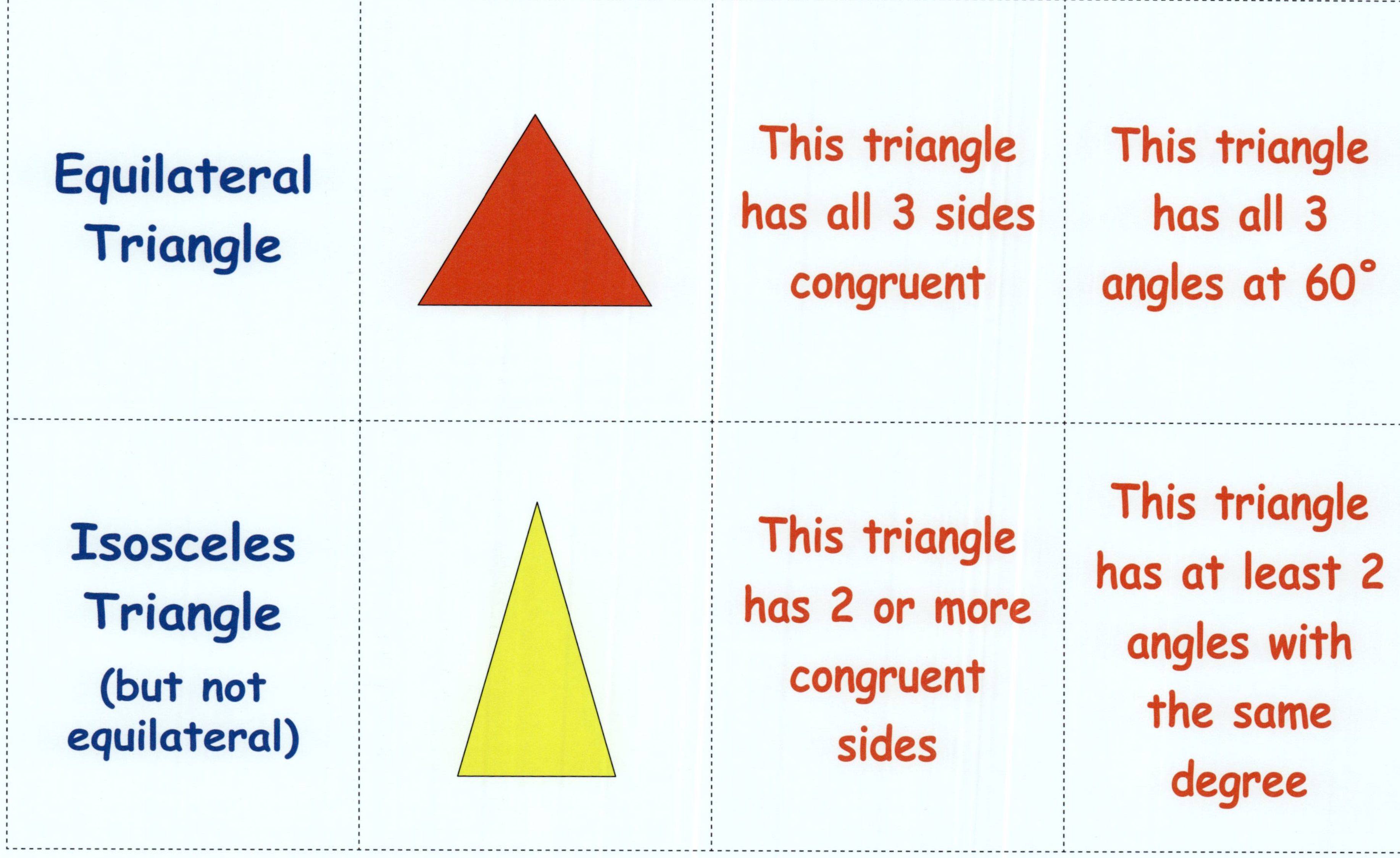
Equilateral Triangle
This triangle has all 3 sides congruent
This triangle has all 3 angles at 60°
Isosceles Triangle (but not equilateral)
This triangle has 2 or more congruent sides
This triangle has at least 2 angles with the same degree

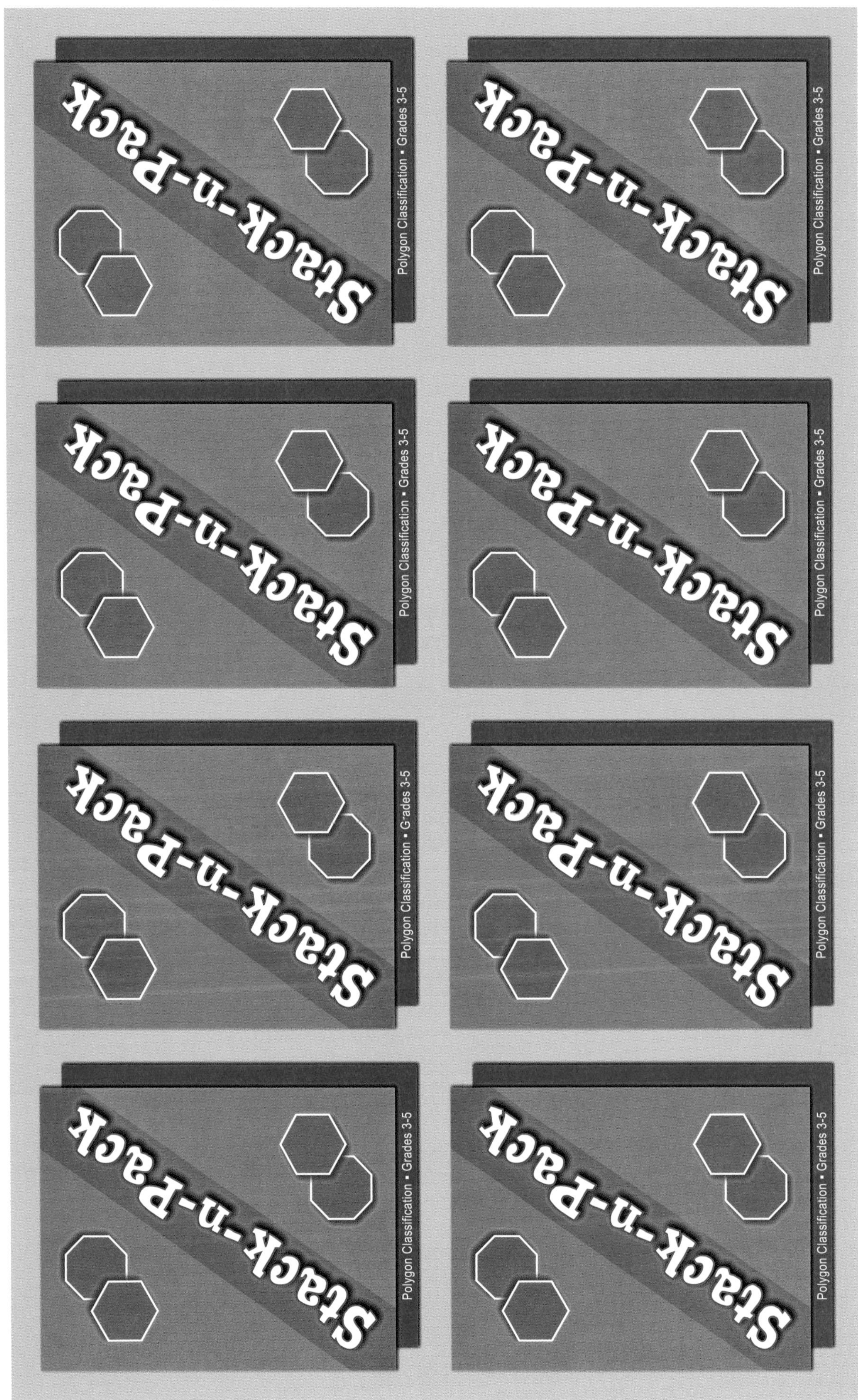
Stack-n-Pack
Polygon Classification ▪ Grades 3-5
Stack-n-Pack
Polygon Classification ▪ Grades 3-5
Stack-n-Pack
Polygon Classification ▪ Grades 3-5
Stack-n-Pack
Polygon Classification ▪ Grades 3-5
Stack-n-Pack
Polygon Classification ▪ G-ades 3-5
Stack-n-Pack
Polygon Classification ▪ Grades 3-5
Stack-n-Pack
Polygon Classification ▪ Grades 3-5
Stack-n-Pack
Polygon Classification ▪ Grades 3-5

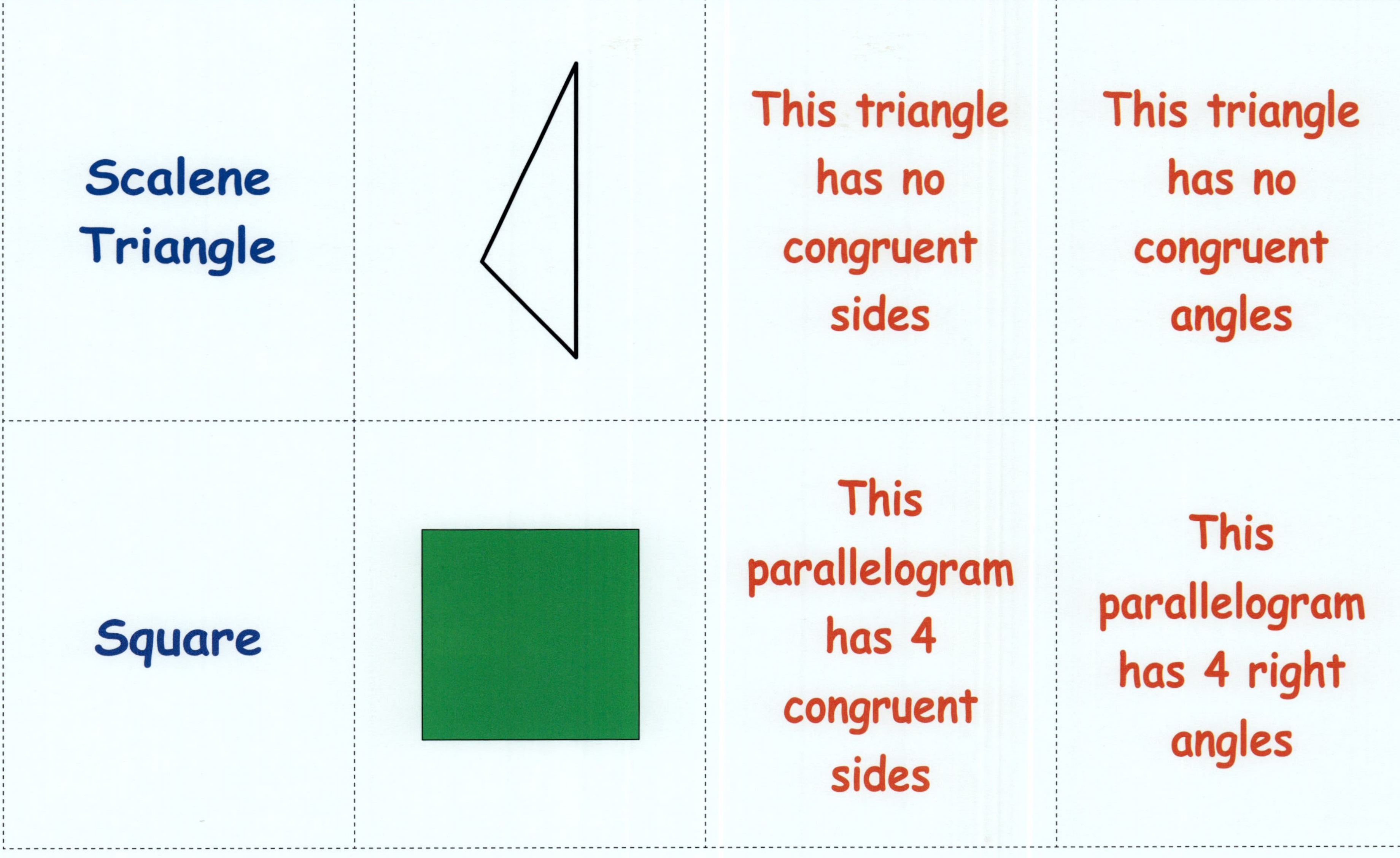
Scalene Triangle
This triangle has no congruent sides
This triangle has no congruent angles
Square
This parallelogram has 4 congruent sides
This parallelogram has 4 right angles

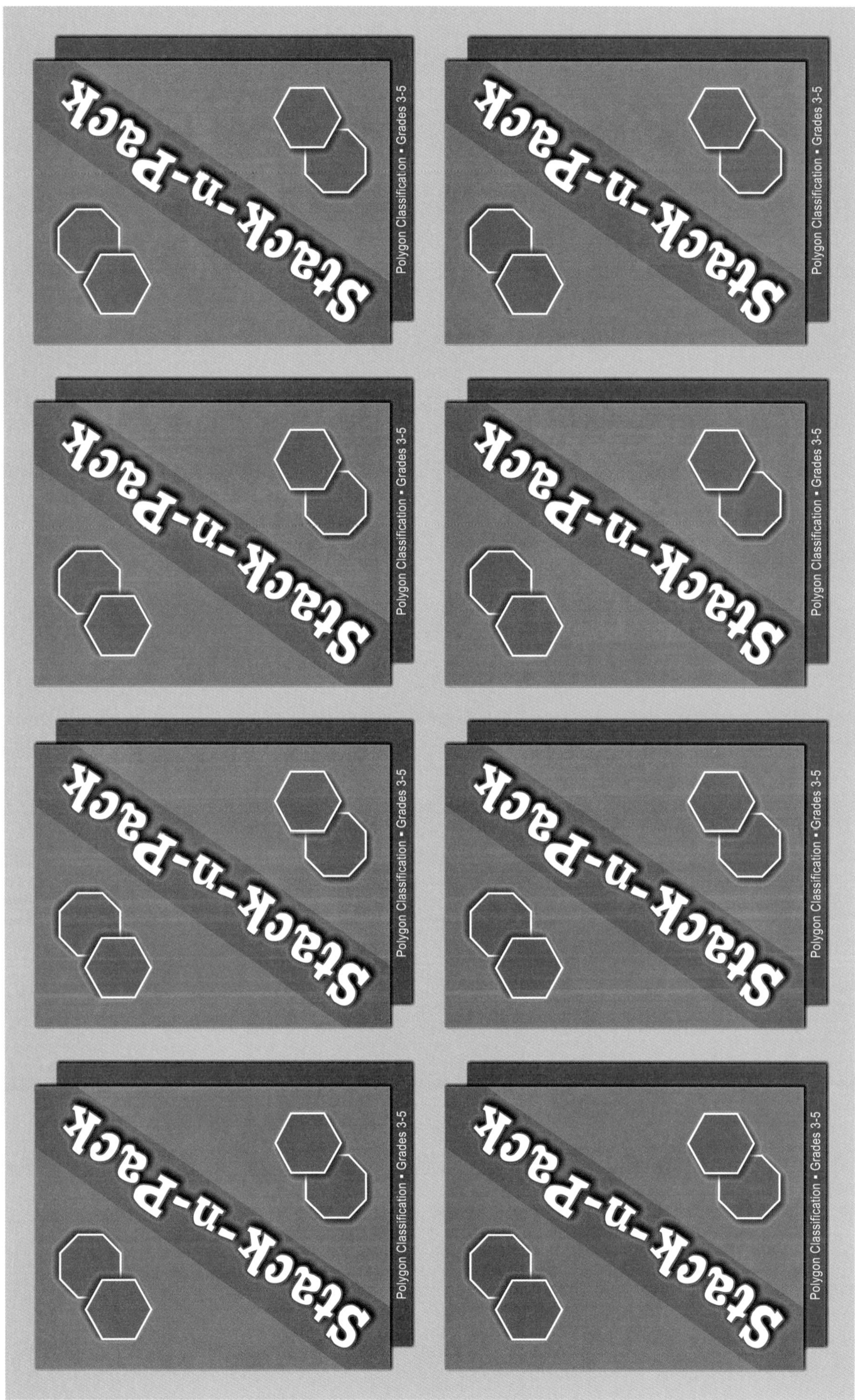
Stack-n-Pack
Polygon Classification ▪ Grades 3-5
Stack-n-Pack
Polygon Classification ▪ Grades 3-5
Stack-n-Pack
Polygon Classification ▪ Grades 3-5
Stack-n-Pack
Polygon Classification ▪ Grades 3-5
Stack-n-Pack
Polygon Classification ▪ Grades 3-5
Stack-n-Pack
Polygon Classification ▪ Grades 3-5
Stack-n-Pack
Polygon Classification ▪ Grades 3-5
Stack-n-Pack
Polygon Classification ▪ Grades 3-5

Rectangle

This parallelogram has 4 sides, but they are not all congruent

This parallelogram has 4 right angles

Parallelogram

This quadrilateral has 2 pairs of parallel sides

This quadrilateral has 2 obtuse and 2 acute angles

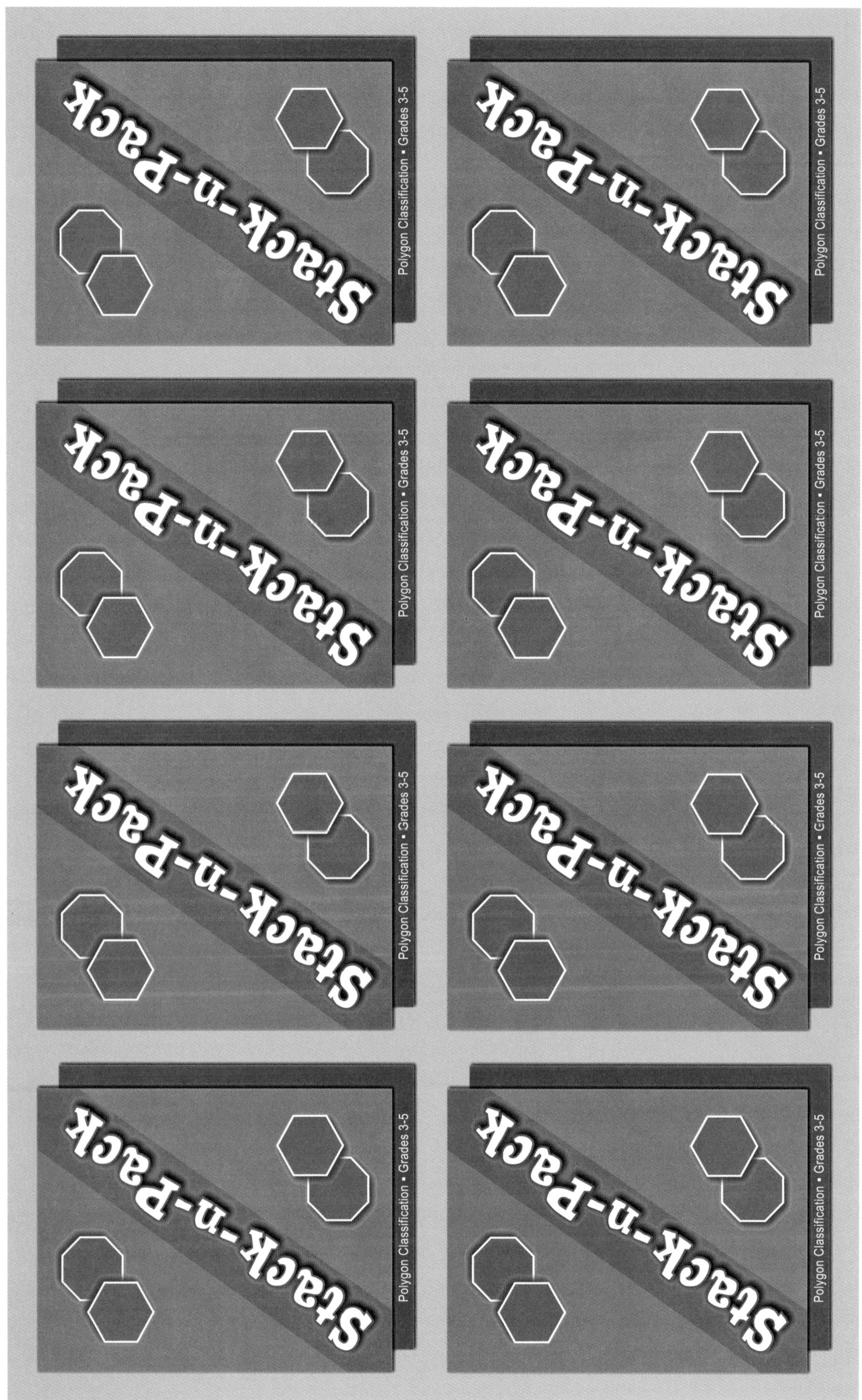
Stack-n-Pack
Polygon Classification ▪ Grades 3-5
Stack-n-Pack
Polygon Classification ▪ Grades 3-5
Stack-n-Pack
Polygon Classification ▪ Grades 3-5
Stack-n-Pack
Polygon Classification ▪ Grades 3-5
Stack-n-Pack
Polygon Classification ▪ Grades 3-5
Stack-n-Pack
Polygon Classification ▪ Grades 3-5
Stack-n-Pack
Polygon Classification ▪ Grades 3-5
Stack-n-Pack
Polygon Classification ▪ Grades 3-5

Rhombus

This parallelogram has 4 congruent sides

This parallelogram has 2 pairs of congruent angles

Trapezoid

This quadrilateral has exactly one pair of parallel sides

This quadrilateral's angles vary with the lengths of the sides

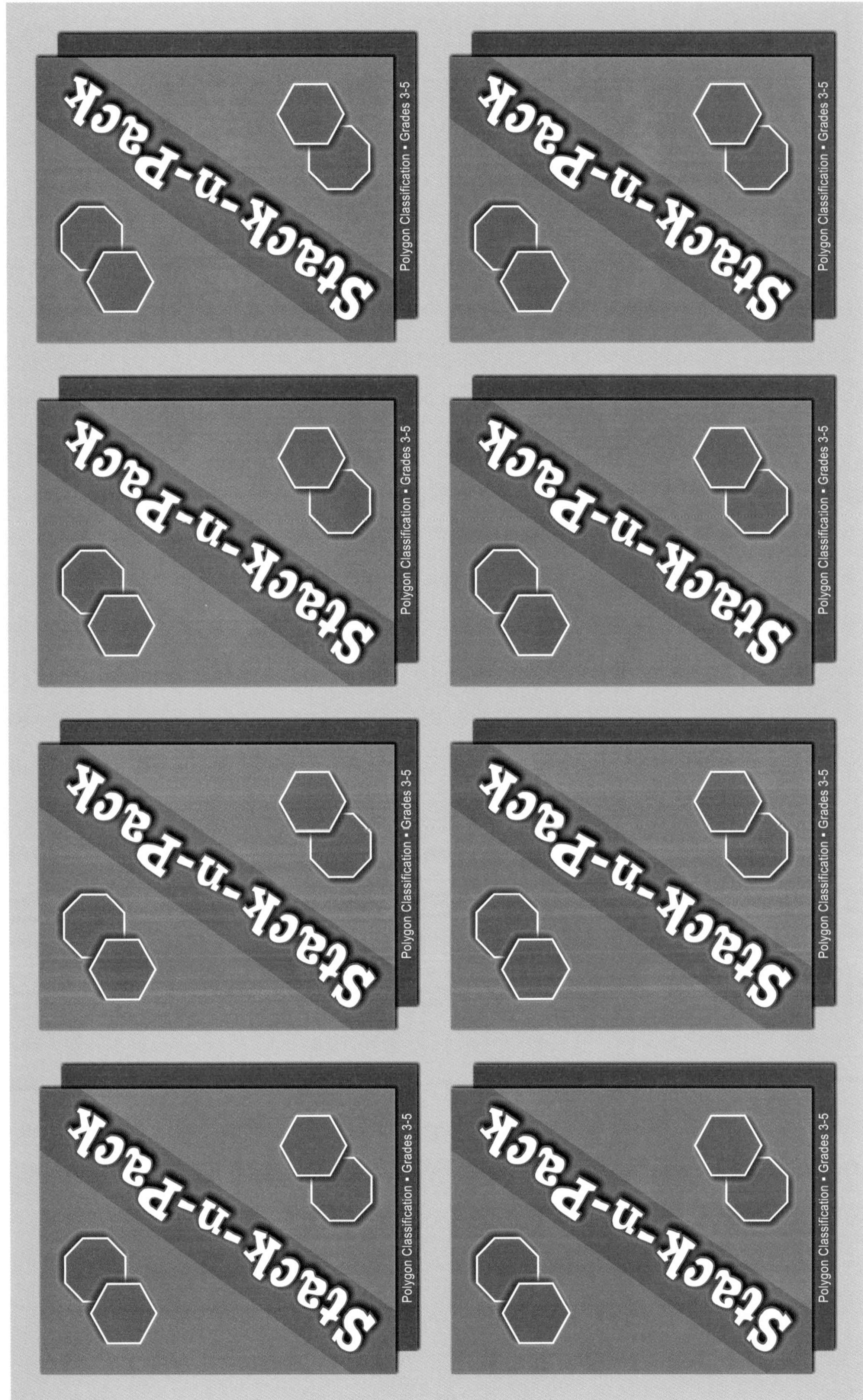
Stack-n-Pack
Polygon Classification ▪ Grades 3-5
Stack-n-Pack
Polygon Classification ▪ Grades 3-5
Stack-n-Pack
Polygon Classification ▪ Grades 3-5
Stack-n-Pack
Polygon Classification ▪ Grades 3-5
Stack-n-Pack
Polygon Classification ▪ Grades 3-5
Stack-n-Pack
Polygon Classification ▪ Grades 3-5
Stack-n-Pack
Polygon Classification ▪ Grades 3-5
Stack-n-Pack
Polygon Classification ▪ Grades 3-5

Regular Pentagon	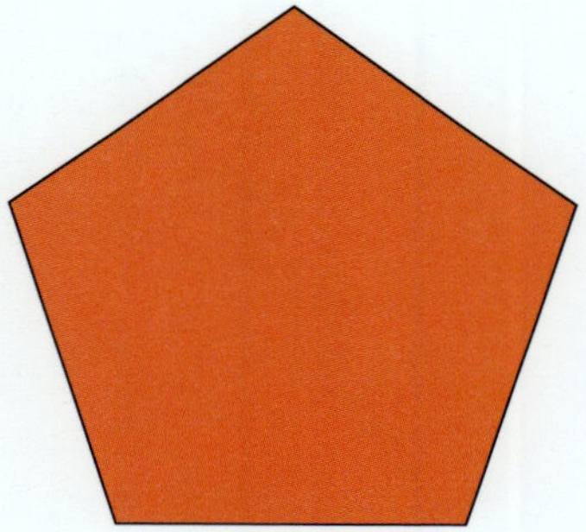	This polygon has 5 congruent sides	Each interior angle of this polygon measures 108°
Regular Hexagon	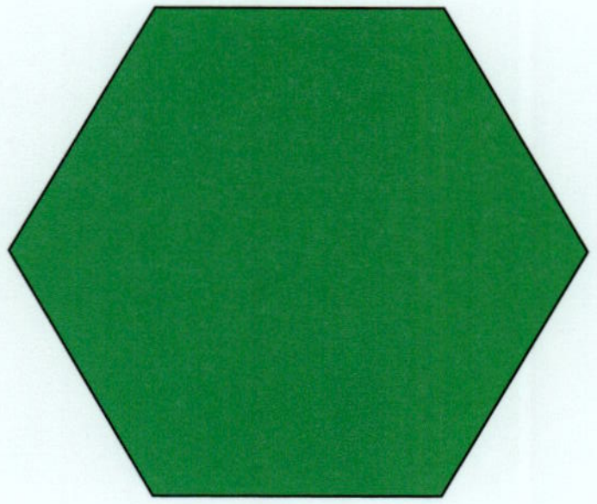	This polygon has 6 congruent sides	Each interior angle of this polygon measures 120°

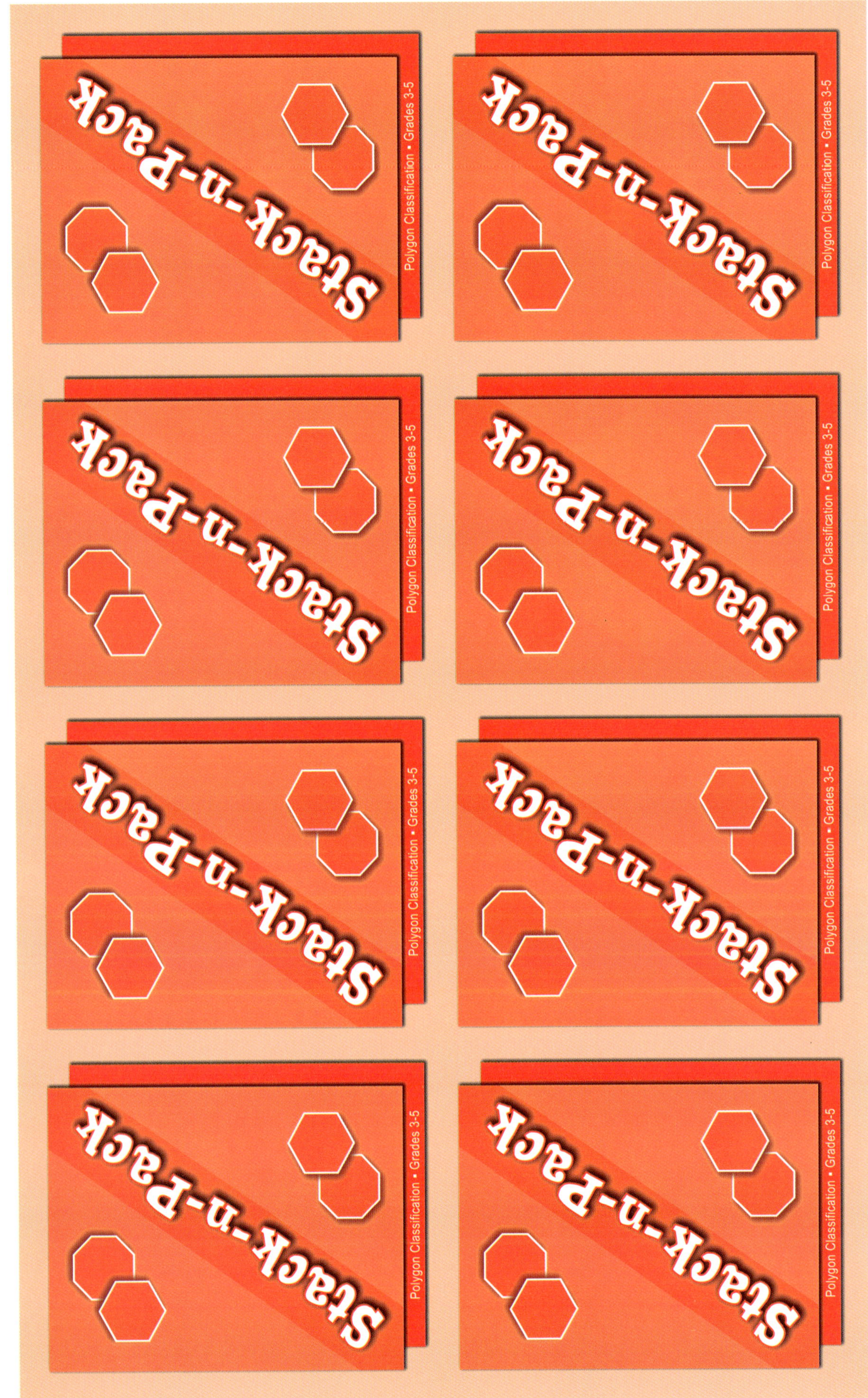
Stack-n-Pack
Polygon Classification • Grades 3-5
Stack-n-Pack
Polygon Classification • Grades 3-5
Stack-n-Pack
Polygon Classification • Grades 3-5
Stack-n-Pack
Polygon Classification • Grades 3-5
Stack-n-Pack
Polygon Classification • Grades 3-5
Stack-n-Pack
Polygon Classification • Grades 3-5
Stack-n-Pack
Polygon Classification • Grades 3-5
Stack-n-Pack
Polygon Classification • Grades 3-5

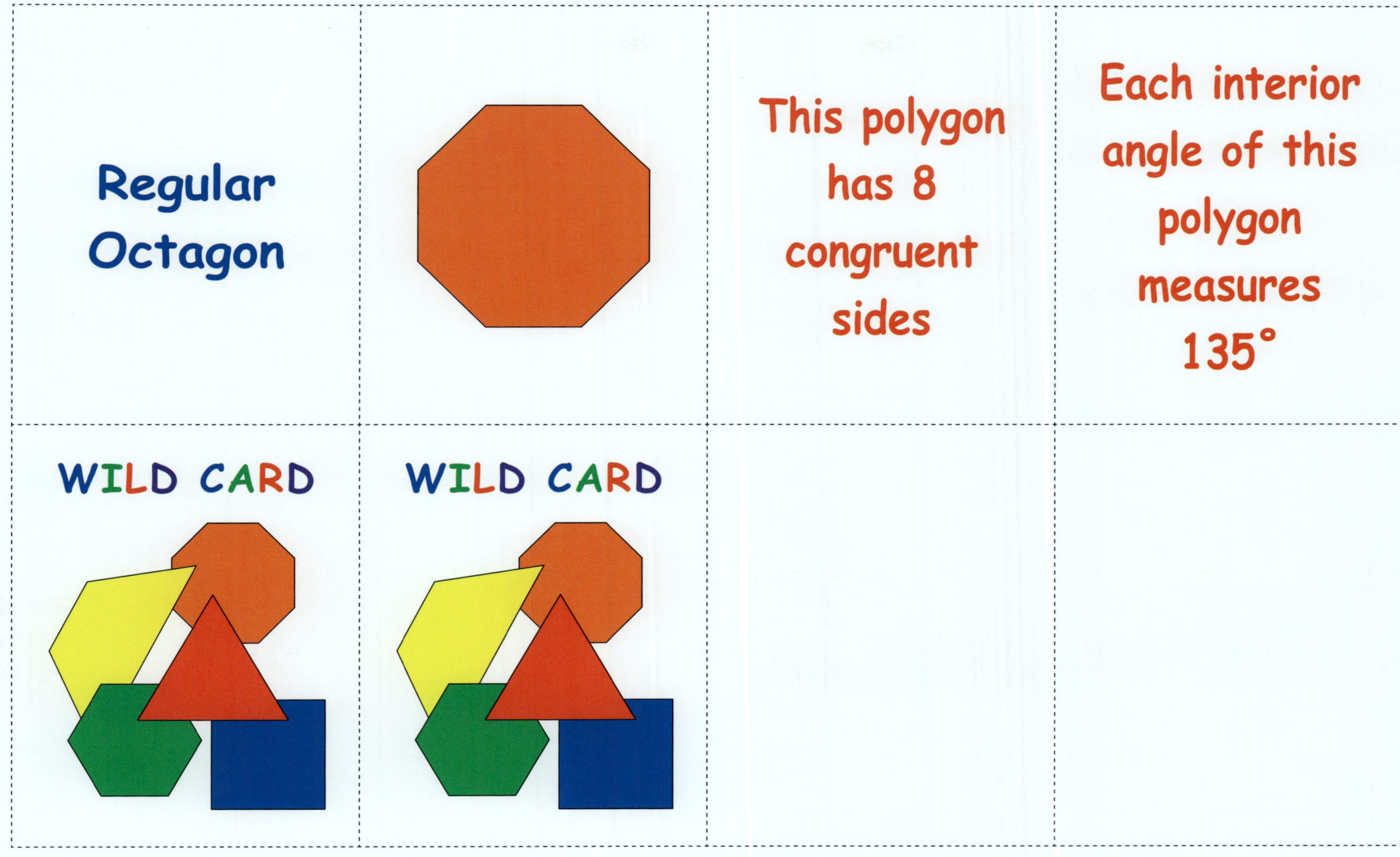
Regular
Octagon
This polygon
has 8
congruent
sides
Each interior
angle of this
polygon
measures
135°
WILD CARD
WILD CARD

Stack-n-Pack
Polygon Classification • Grades 3-5
Stack-n-Pack
Polygon Classification • Grades 3-5
Stack-n-Pack
Polygon Classification • Grades 3-5
Stack-n-Pack
Polygon Classification • Grades 3-5
Stack-n-Pack
Polygon Classification • Grades 3-5
Stack-n-Pack
Polygon Classification • Grades 3-5
Stack-n-Pack
Polygon Classification • Grades 3-5
Stack-n-Pack
Polygon Classification • Grades 3-5

LCM and GCF

Stack-n-Pack	Stack Starter	# of Cards in Completed Stack	Cards in the Completed Stack
LCM and GCF	Set of Numbers (4 and 5; 3, 6 and 8; ...)	3	Set of 2 or 3 Numbers, GCF, LCM

Note: The Stack Starter is in blue.

Directions for Playing "Stack-n-Pack"

1. Form groups of 3-4 players.
2. Each player is dealt 4 cards. The remaining cards are placed face down in the center of the table. This is the draw pile. There is no discard pile.
3. Play begins with the person to the left of the dealer and continues clockwise around the table.
4. The first player can start a stack with the appropriate stack starter card (see Stack-n-Pack Information Chart above). This is NOT his/her stack. Any player can play on any stack. Once a stack has been started, the other cards in the stack may be played in any order. After playing his/her card, the first player draws a card from the draw pile ending his/her turn. If the first player does not have a stack starter, then he/she must PASS.

(Directions continued on back)

5. The next player has the option of playing on any stack laid on the table or beginning a new stack. Only ONE (1) card can be played at each turn. After playing his/her card, the player draws a card from the draw pile ending his/her turn.

6. Play continues in this manner with each player either playing on a stack or beginning a new one. Players must play if they are able. Otherwise, they must pass and lose their turn. Players must also remember to draw after they play their card.

7. A completed stack contains the total number of cards and representations described in the Stack-n-Pack Information Chart. The number of cards and representations necessary to complete a stack varies with each game. The player who completes the stack by playing the final card wins that stack.

8. Once all the cards have been drawn, play continues until no more cards can be played.

9. The game is over when the last stack has been completed. The player with the most stacks is the winner.

10, 15	6, 8
8, 24	3, 9
6, 36	4, 32
14, 21	5, 6

Stack-n-Pack
LCM
GCF
LCM
GCF
LCM and GCF ▪ Grades 3-5

LCM = 30

LCM = 24

LCM = 24

LCM = 9

LCM = 36

LCM = 32

LCM = 42

LCM = 30

Stack-n-Pack
LCM
GCF
LCM
GCF
LCM and GCF ▪ Grades 3-5

GCF = 5

GCF = 2

GCF = 8

GCF = 3

GCF = 6

GCF = 4

GCF = 7

GCF = 1

Stack-n-Pack
LCM
GCF
LCM and GCF ▪ Grades 3-5

2, 4, 11	20, 10, 60
6, 4, 18	6, 15, 3
3, 4, 6	16, 32, 4
7, 21, 42	64, 32, 16

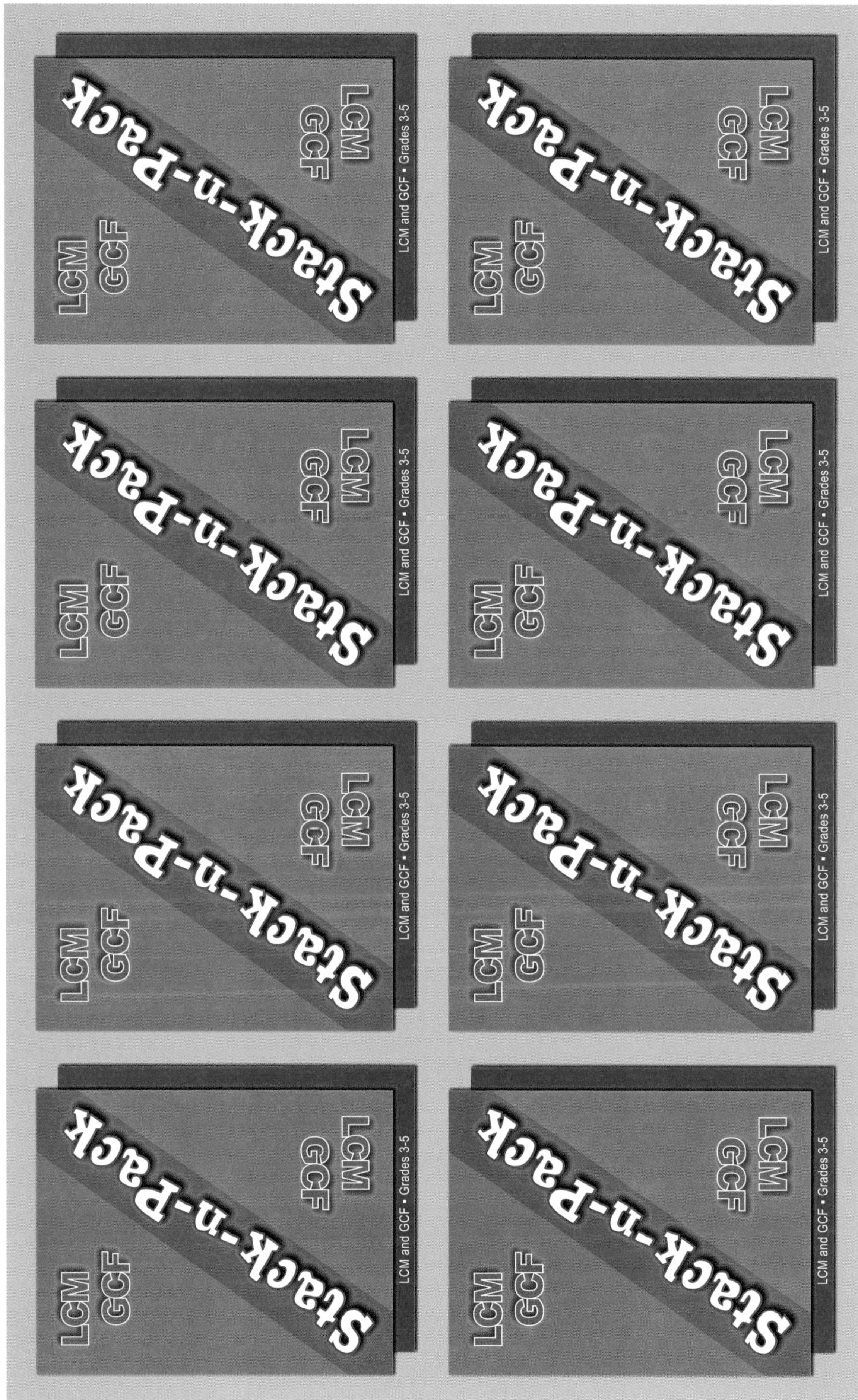
Stack-n-Pack
LCM
GCF
LCM and GCF ▪ Grades 3-5

LCM = 44	LCM = 60
LCM = 36	LCM = 30
LCM = 12	LCM = 32
LCM = 42	LCM = 64

Stack-n-Pack
LCM
GCF
LCM
GCF
LCM and GCF • Grades 3-5

GCF = 1

GCF = 10

GCF = 2

GCF = 3

GCF = 1

GCF = 4

GCF = 7

GCF = 16

Stack-n-Pack
LCM
GCF
LCM
GCF
LCM and GCF • Grades 3-5

LCM
WILD CARD
GCF

LCM
WILD CARD
GCF

Stack-n-Pack
LCM
GCF
LCM
GCF
LCM and GCF • Grades 3-5

Equivalent Fractions

Stack-n-Pack	Stack Starter	# of Cards in Completed Stack	Cards in the Completed Stack
Equivalent Fractions	Simplified Fraction ($\frac{1}{2}$, $\frac{1}{4}$, ...)	4	Simplified Fraction, Equivalent Fraction in Fraction Form, as Part of a Rectangle, as Part of a Set

Note: The Stack Starter is in blue.

Directions for Playing "Stack-n-Pack"

1. Form groups of 3-4 players.
2. Each player is dealt 4 cards. The remaining cards are placed face down in the center of the table. This is the draw pile. There is no discard pile.
3. Play begins with the person to the left of the dealer and continues clockwise around the table.
4. The first player can start a stack with the appropriate stack starter card (see Stack-n-Pack Information Chart above). This is NOT his/her stack. Any player can play on any stack. Once a stack has been started, the other cards in the stack may be played in any order. After playing his/her card, the first player draws a card from the draw pile ending his/her turn. If the first player does not have a stack starter, then he/she must PASS.

(Directions continued on back)

5. The next player has the option of playing on any stack laid on the table or beginning a new stack. Only ONE (1) card can be played at each turn. After playing his/her card, the player draws a card from the draw pile ending his/her turn.

6. Play continues in this manner with each player either playing on a stack or beginning a new one. Players must play if they are able. Otherwise, they must pass and lose their turn. Players must also remember to draw after they play their card.

7. A completed stack contains the total number of cards and representations described in the Stack-n-Pack Information Chart. The number of cards and representations necessary to complete a stack varies with each game. The player who completes the stack by playing the final card wins that stack.

8. Once all the cards have been drawn, play continues until no more cards can be played.

9. The game is over when the last stack has been completed. The player with the most stacks is the winner.

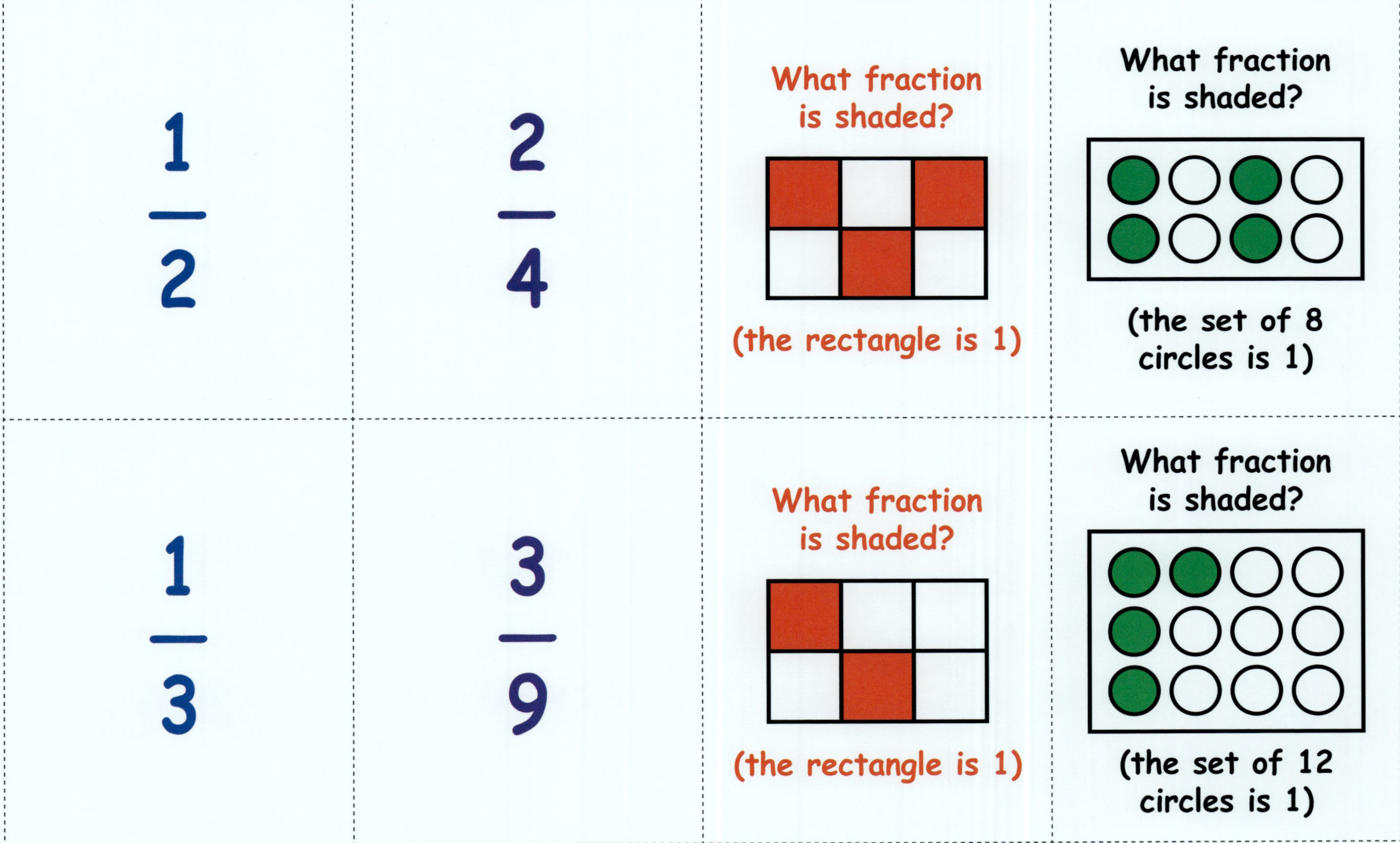
1/2
2/4
What fraction is shaded?
(the rectangle is 1)
What fraction is shaded?
(the set of 8 circles is 1)
1/3
3/9
What fraction is shaded?
(the rectangle is 1)
What fraction is shaded?
(the set of 12 circles is 1)

Stack-n-Pack
Equivalent Fractions ▪ Grades 3-5
Stack-n-Pack
Equivalent Fractions ▪ Grades 3-5
Stack-n-Pack
Equivalent Fractions ▪ Grades 3-5
Stack-n-Pack
Equivalent Fractions ▪ Grades 3-5
Stack-n-Pack
Equivalent Fractions ▪ Grades 3-5
Stack-n-Pack
Equivalent Fractions ▪ Grades 3-5
Stack-n-Pack
Equivalent Fractions ▪ Grades 3-5
Stack-n-Pack
Equivalent Fractions ▪ Grades 3-5

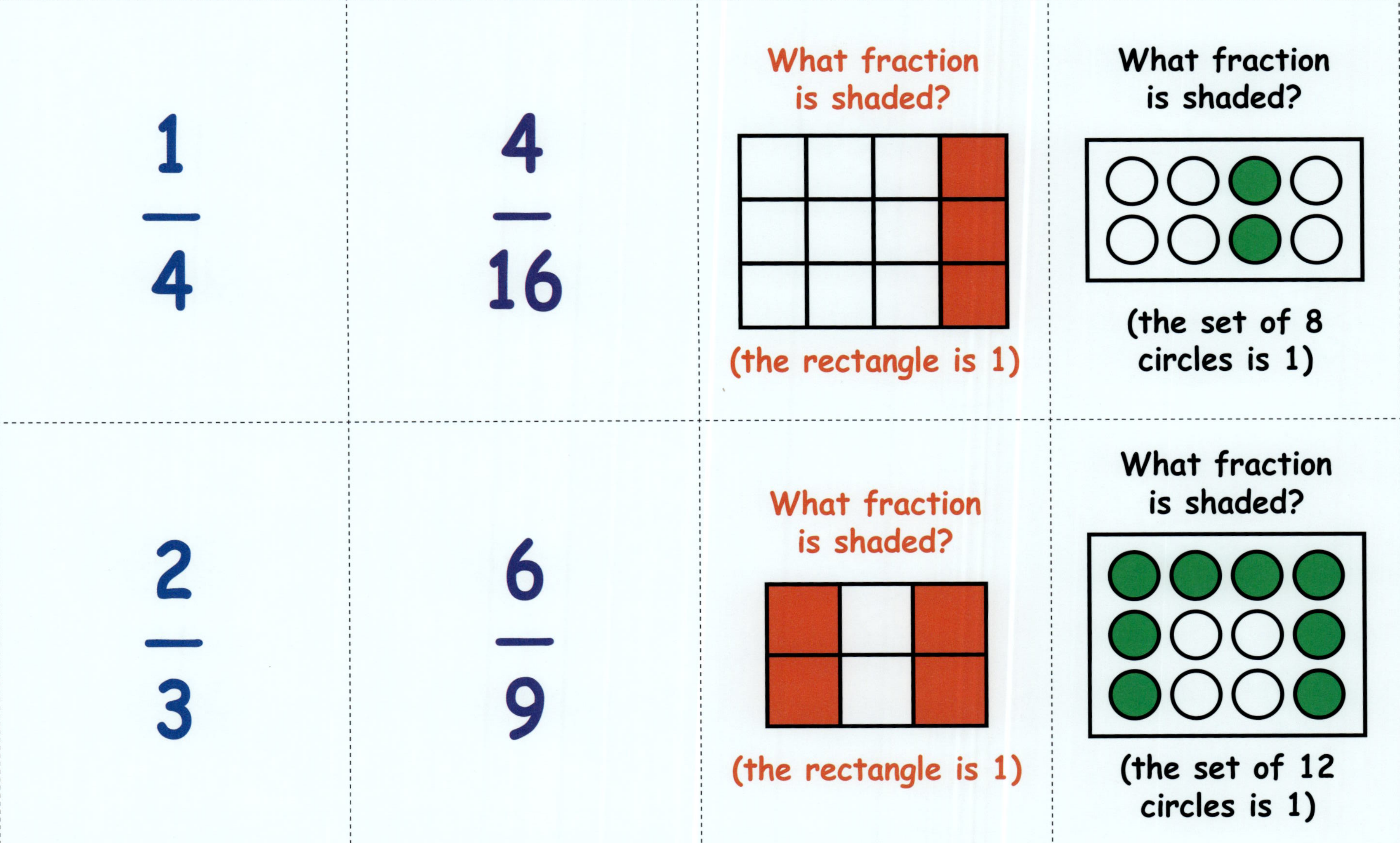

1/4
4/16
What fraction is shaded?
(the rectangle is 1)
What fraction is shaded?
(the set of 8 circles is 1)
2/3
6/9
What fraction is shaded?
(the rectangle is 1)
What fraction is shaded?
(the set of 12 circles is 1)

Stack-n-Pack
Equivalent Fractions ▪ Grades 3-5
Stack-n-Pack
Equivalent Fractions ▪ Grades 3-5
Stack-n-Pack
Equivalent Fractions ▪ Grades 3-5
Stack-n-Pack
Equivalent Fractions ▪ Grades 3-5
Stack-n-Pack
Equivalent Fractions ▪ Grades 3-5
Stack-n-Pack
Equivalent Fractions ▪ Grades 3-5
Stack-n-Pack
Equivalent Fractions ▪ Grades 3-5
Stack-n-Pack
Equivalent Fractions ▪ Grades 3-5

$\frac{3}{5}$

$\frac{3}{4}$

$\frac{12}{20}$

$\frac{12}{16}$

What fraction is shaded?

(the rectangle is 1)

What fraction is shaded?

(the rectangle is 1)

What fraction is shaded?

(the set of 15 circles is 1)

What fraction is shaded?

(the set of 8 circles is 1)

Stack-n-Pack
Equivalent Fractions ▪ Grades 3-5
Stack-n-Pack
Equivalent Fractions ▪ Grades 3-5
Stack-n-Pack
Equivalent Fractions ▪ Grades 3-5
Stack-n-Pack
Equivalent Fractions ▪ Grades 3-5
Stack-n-Pack
Equivalent Fractions ▪ Grades 3-5
Stack-n-Pack
Equivalent Fractions ▪ Grades 3-5
Stack-n-Pack
Equivalent Fractions ▪ Grades 3-5
Stack-n-Pack
Equivalent Fractions ▪ Grades 3-5

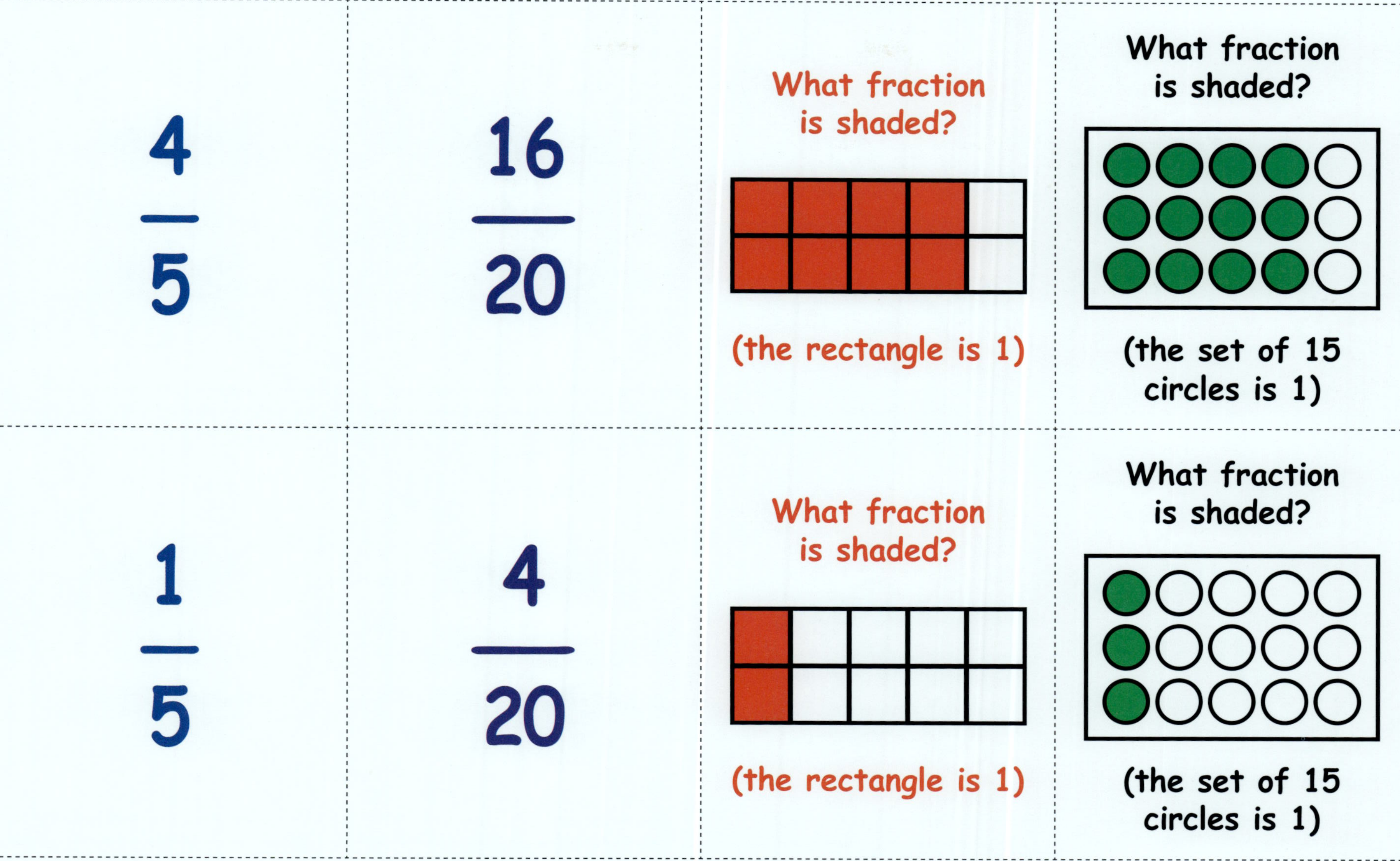
4/5
16/20
What fraction is shaded?
(the rectangle is 1)
What fraction is shaded?
(the set of 15 circles is 1)
1/5
4/20
What fraction is shaded?
(the rectangle is 1)
What fraction is shaded?
(the set of 15 circles is 1)

Stack-n-Pack
Equivalent Fractions • Grades 3-5

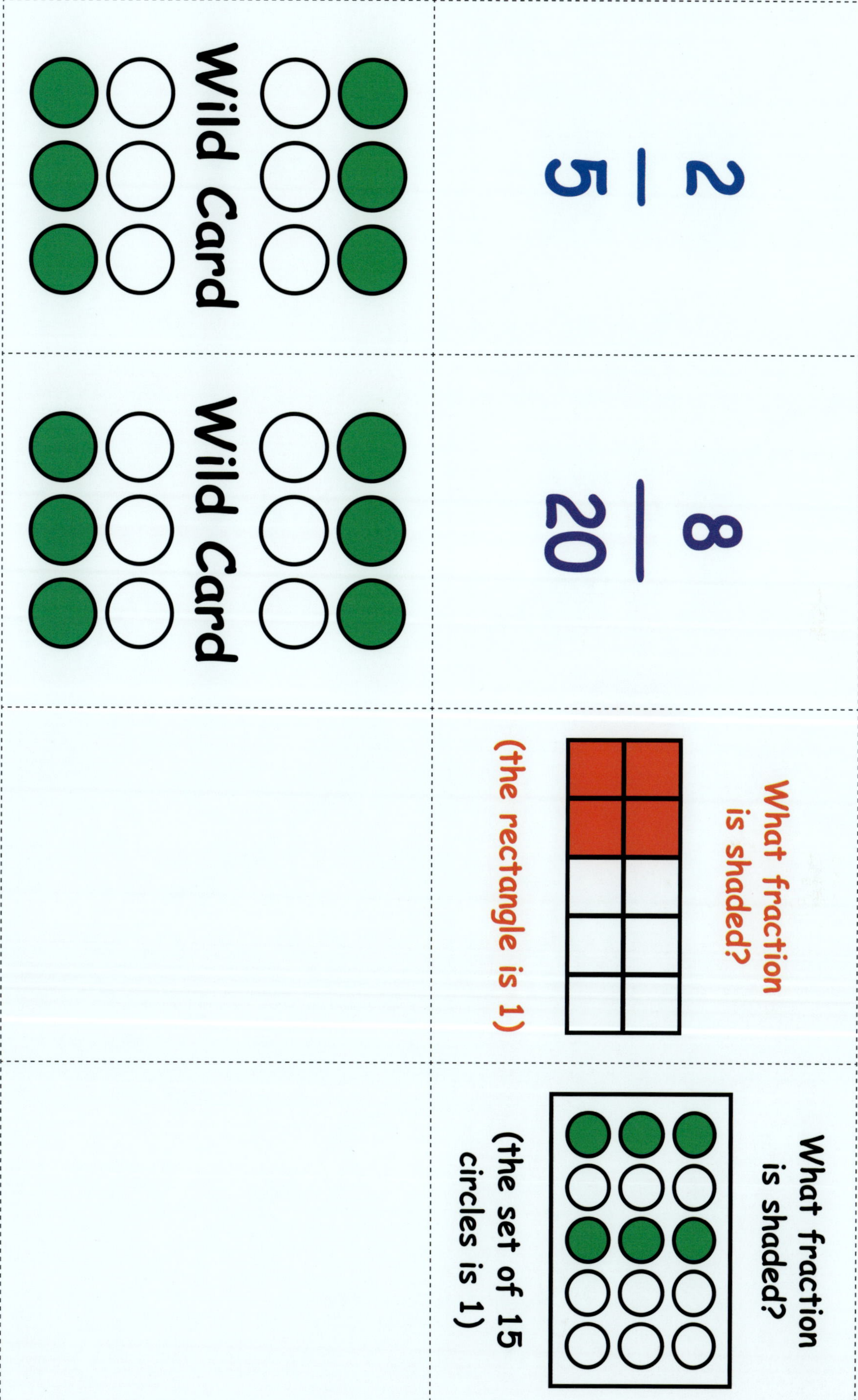
Wild Card
2/5
Wild Card
8/20
What fraction is shaded?
(the rectangle is 1)
What fraction is shaded?
(the set of 15 circles is 1)

Stack-n-Pack
Equivalent Fractions ▪ Grades 3-5
Stack-n-Pack
Equivalent Fractions ▪ Grades 3-5
Stack-n-Pack
Equivalent Fractions ▪ Grades 3-5
Stack-n-Pack
Equivalent Fractions ▪ Grades 3-5
Stack-n-Pack
Equivalent Fractions ▪ Grades 3-5
Stack-n-Pack
Equivalent Fractions ▪ Grades 3-5
Stack-n-Pack
Equivalent Fractions ▪ Grades 3-5
Stack-n-Pack
Equivalent Fractions ▪ Grades 3-5

Addition & Multiplication Properties

Stack-n-Pack	Stack Starter	# of Cards in Completed Stack	Cards in the Completed Stack
Addition & Multiplication Properties	Property Name (identity, commutative, ...)	4	Property Name, Variable Representation, 2 Examples

Note: The Stack Starter is in blue.

Directions for Playing "Stack-n-Pack"

1. Form groups of 3-4 players.
2. Each player is dealt 4 cards. The remaining cards are placed face down in the center of the table. This is the draw pile. There is no discard pile.
3. Play begins with the person to the left of the dealer and continues clockwise around the table.
4. The first player can start a stack with the appropriate stack starter card (see Stack-n-Pack Information Chart above). This is NOT his/her stack. Any player can play on any stack. Once a stack has been started, the other cards in the stack may be played in any order. After playing his/her card, the first player draws a card from the draw pile ending his/her turn. If the first player does not have a stack starter, then he/she must PASS.

(Directions continued on back)

5. The next player has the option of playing on any stack laid on the table or beginning a new stack. Only ONE (1) card can be played at each turn. After playing his/her card, the player draws a card from the draw pile ending his/her turn.

6. Play continues in this manner with each player either playing on a stack or beginning a new one. Players must play if they are able. Otherwise, they must pass and lose their turn. Players must also remember to draw after they play their card.

7. A completed stack contains the total number of cards and representations described in the Stack-n-Pack Information Chart. The number of cards and representations necessary to complete a stack varies with each game. The player who completes the stack by playing the final card wins that stack.

8. Once all the cards have been drawn, play continues until no more cards can be played.

9. The game is over when the last stack has been completed. The player with the most stacks is the winner.

Commutative Property of Addition	$a+b = b+a$	$3+5 = 5+3$	$43+95 = 95+43$
Associative Property of Addition	$a+(b+c) = (a+b)+c$	$3+(2+6) = (3+2)+6$	$15+(10+43) = (15+10)+43$

Stack-n-Pack
a+b = b+a
Addition & Multiplication Properties • Grades 3-5
Stack-n-Pack
a+b = b+a
Addition & Multiplication Properties • Grades 3-5
Stack-n-Pack
a+b = b+a
Addition & Multiplication Properties • Grades 3-5
Stack-n-Pack
a+b = b+a
Addition & Multiplication Properties • Grades 3-5
Stack-n-Pack
a+b = b+a
Addition & Multiplication Properties • Grades 3-5
Stack-n-Pack
a+b = b+a
Addition & Multiplication Properties • Grades 3-5
Stack-n-Pack
a+b = b+a
Addition & Multiplication Properties • Grades 3-5
Stack-n-Pack
a+b = b+a
Addition & Multiplication Properties • Grades 3-5

Additive Identity Property	$a + 0 = a$	$8 + 0 = 8$	$33 + 0 = 33$
Distributive Property	$a(c+b) =$ $ac+ab$	$7(4+8) =$ $7(4)+7(8)$	$8(2+25) =$ $8(2)+8(25)$

Stack-n-Pack
a+b = b+a
Addition & Multiplication Properties ▪ Grades 3-5
Stack-n-Pack
a+b = b+a
Addition & Multiplication Properties ▪ Grades 3-5
Stack-n-Pack
a+b = b+a
Addition & Multiplication Properties ▪ Grades 3-5
Stack-n-Pack
a+b = b+a
Addition & Multiplication Properties ▪ Grades 3-5
Stack-n-Pack
a+b = b+a
Addition & Multiplication Properties ▪ Grades 3-5
Stack-n-Pack
a+b = b+a
Addition & Multiplication Properties ▪ Grades 3-5
Stack-n-Pack
a+b = b+a
Addition & Multiplication Properties ▪ Grades 3-5
Stack-n-Pack
a+b = b+a
Addition & Multiplication Properties ▪ Grades 3-5

Associative Property of Multiplication	$a \cdot (b \cdot c) = (a \cdot b) \cdot c$	$7 \cdot (2 \cdot 5) = (7 \cdot 2) \cdot 5$	$21 \cdot (14 \cdot 50) = (21 \cdot 14) \cdot 50$
Multiplicative Identity Property	$a \cdot 1 = a$	$4 \cdot 1 = 4$	$65 \cdot 1 = 65$

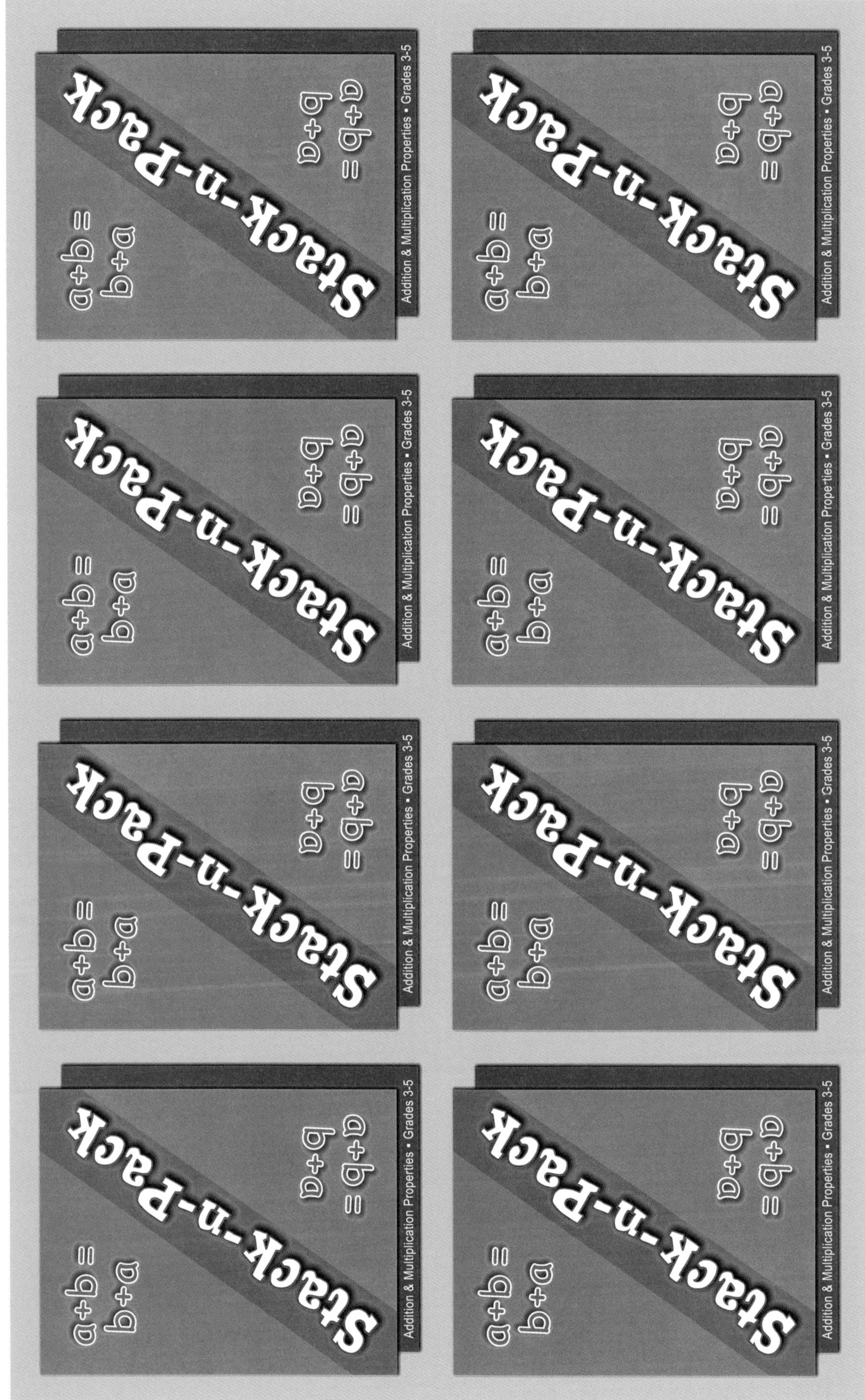
Stack-n-Pack
a+b = b+a
a+b = b+a
Addition & Multiplication Properties • Grades 3-5
Stack-n-Pack
a+b = b+a
a+b = b+a
Addition & Multiplication Properties • Grades 3-5
Stack-n-Pack
a+b = b+a
a+b = b+a
Addition & Multiplication Properties • Grades 3-5
Stack-n-Pack
a+b = b+a
a+b = b+a
Addition & Multiplication Properties • Grades 3-5
Stack-n-Pack
a+b = b+a
a+b = b+a
Addition & Multiplication Properties • Grades 3-5
Stack-n-Pack
a+b = b+a
a+b = b+a
Addition & Multiplication Properties • Grades 3-5
Stack-n-Pack
a+b = b+a
a+b = b+a
Addition & Multiplication Properties • Grades 3-5
Stack-n-Pack
a+b = b+a
a+b = b+a
Addition & Multiplication Properties • Grades 3-5

Commutative Property of Multiplication	$a \cdot b = b \cdot a$	$5 \cdot 7 = 7 \cdot 5$	$22 \cdot 18 = 18 \cdot 22$
Zero Product Property	$a \cdot b = 0$, then $a = 0$ or $b = 0$	$5 \cdot 0 = 0$	$0 \cdot 84 = 0$

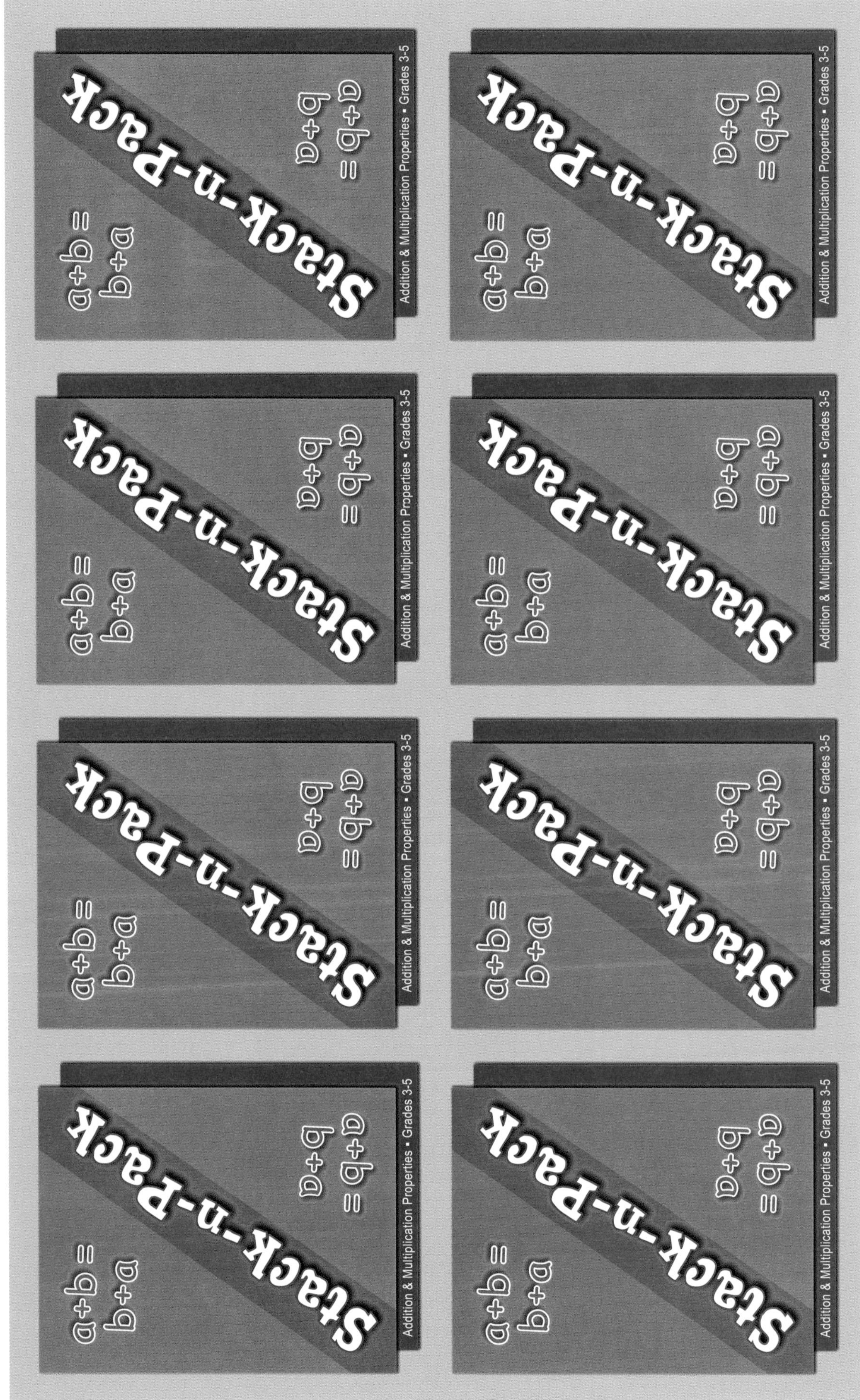
Stack-n-Pack
a+b = b+a
a+b = b+a
Addition & Multiplication Properties ▪ Grades 3-5

a+b = b+a
Wild
Card
a•1 = a
a+b = b+a
Wild
Card
a•1 = a

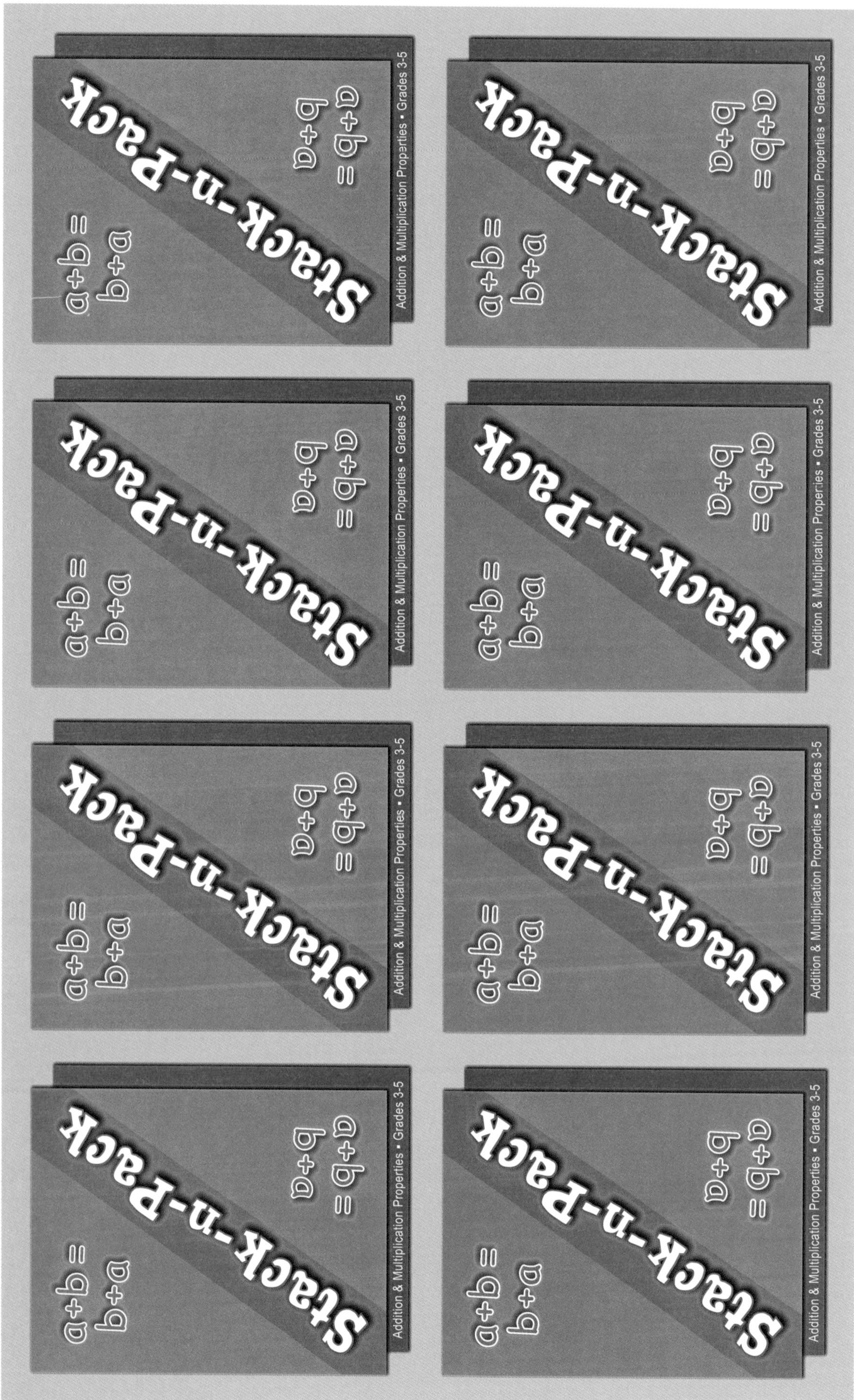
Stack-n-Pack
a+b = b+a
Addition & Multiplication Properties • Grades 3-5

Line Geometry

Stack-n-Pack	Stack Starter	# of Cards in Completed Stack	Cards in the Completed Stack
Line Geometry	Geometric Term (ray, line, ...)	4	Name, Definition, 2 Pictorial Representations

Note: The Stack Starter is in blue.

Directions for Playing "Stack-n-Pack"

1. Form groups of 3-4 players.
2. Each player is dealt 4 cards. The remaining cards are placed face down in the center of the table. This is the draw pile. There is no discard pile.
3. Play begins with the person to the left of the dealer and continues clockwise around the table.
4. The first player can start a stack with the appropriate stack starter card (see Stack-n-Pack Information Chart above). This is NOT his/her stack. Any player can play on any stack. Once a stack has been started, the other cards in the stack may be played in any order. After playing his/her card, the first player draws a card from the draw pile ending his/her turn. If the first player does not have a stack starter, then he/she must PASS.

(Directions continued on back)

5. The next player has the option of playing on any stack laid on the table or beginning a new stack. Only ONE (1) card can be played at each turn. After playing his/her card, the player draws a card from the draw pile ending his/her turn.

6. Play continues in this manner with each player either playing on a stack or beginning a new one. Players must play if they are able. Otherwise, they must pass and lose their turn. Players must also remember to draw after they play their card.

7. A completed stack contains the total number of cards and representations described in the Stack-n-Pack Information Chart. The number of cards and representations necessary to complete a stack varies with each game. The player who completes the stack by playing the final card wins that stack.

8. Once all the cards have been drawn, play continues until no more cards can be played.

9. The game is over when the last stack has been completed. The player with the most stacks is the winner.

Line Segment

Parallel Lines

Ray

Perpendicular Lines

Diameter

Intersecting Lines (non-perpendicular)

Radius

Line

Stack-n-Pack
Line Geometry ▪ Grades 3-5
Stack-n-Pack
Line Geometry ▪ Grades 3-5
Stack-n-Pack
Line Geometry ▪ Grades 3-5
Stack-n-Pack
Line Geometry ▪ Graces 3-5
Stack-n-Pack
Line Geometry ▪ Grades 3-5
Stack-n-Pack
Line Geometry ▪ Grades 3-5
Stack-n-Pack
Line Geometry ▪ Grades 3-5
Stack-n-Pack
Line Geometry ▪ Grades 3-5

Chord
(but, it is not
a diameter)

Vertex

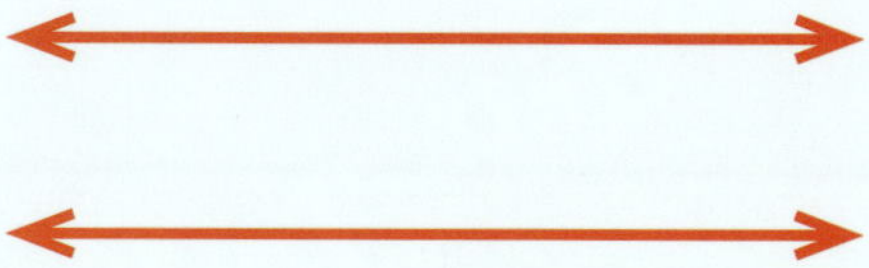

Acute
Angle

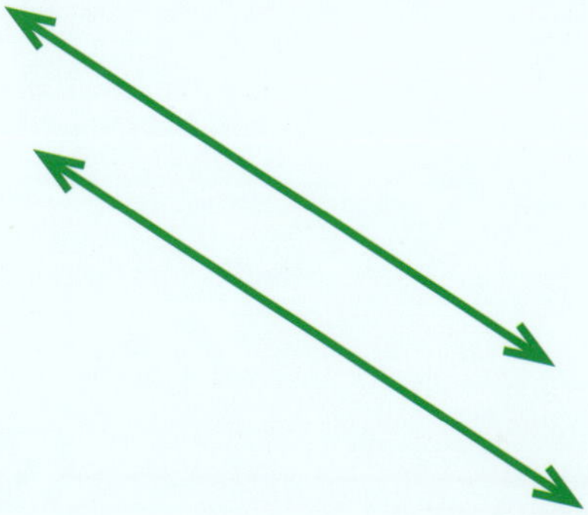

Obtuse
Angle

Right
Angle

Straight
Angle

Stack-n-Pack
Line Geometry ▪ Grades 3-5
Stack-n-Pack
Line Geometry ▪ Grades 3-5
Stack-n-Pack
Line Geometry ▪ Grades 3-5
Stack-n-Pack
Line Geometry ▪ Grades 3-5
Stack-n-Pack
Line Geometry ▪ Graces 3-5
Stack-n-Pack
Line Geometry ▪ Grades 3-5
Stack-n-Pack
Line Geometry ▪ Grades 3-5
Stack-n-Pack
Line Geometry ▪ Grades 3-5

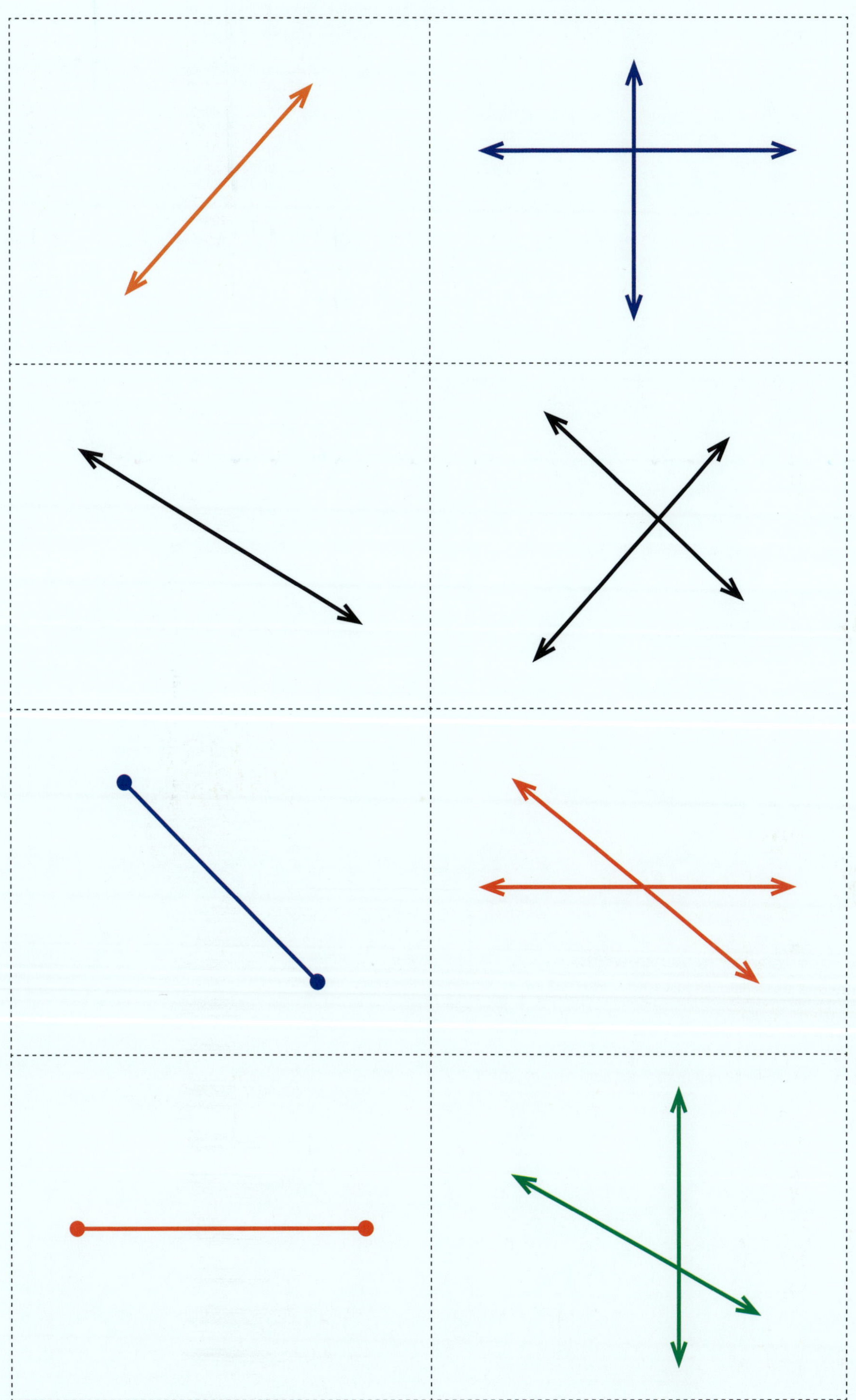

Stack-n-Pack
Line Geometry • Grades 3-5
Stack-n-Pack
Line Geometry • Grades 3-5
Stack-n-Pack
Line Geometry • Grades 3-5
Stack-n-Pack
Line Geometry • Grades 3-5
Stack-n-Pack
Line Geometry • Grades 3-5
Stack-n-Pack
Line Geometry • Grades 3-5
Stack-n-Pack
Line Geometry • Grades 3-5
Stack-n-Pack
Line Geometry • Grades 3-5

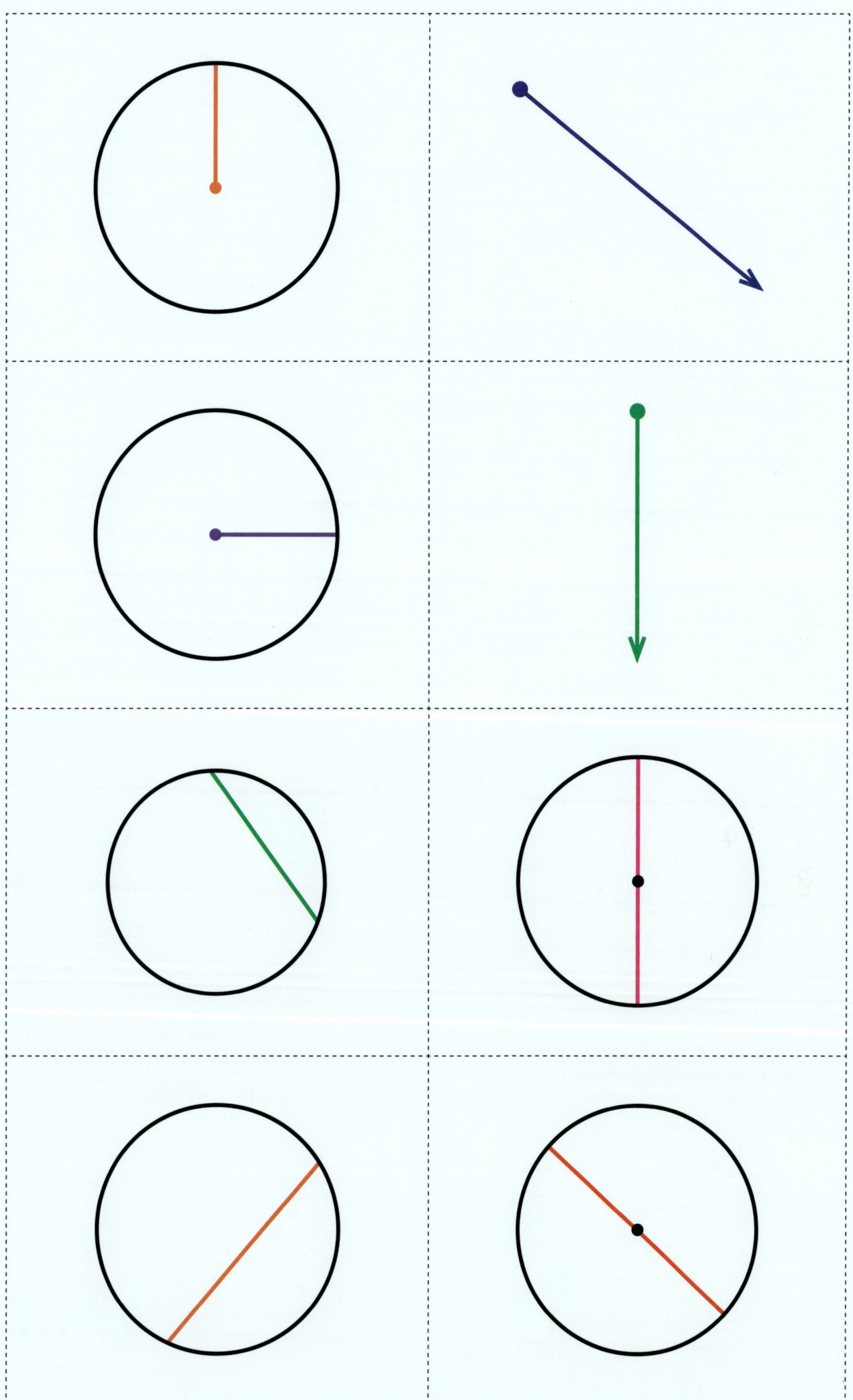

Stack-n-Pack
Line Geometry ▪ Grades 3-5
Stack-n-Pack
Line Geometry ▪ Grades 3-5
Stack-n-Pack
Line Geometry ▪ Grades 3-5
Stack-n-Pack
Line Geometry ▪ Grades 3-5
Stack-n-Pack
Line Geometry ▪ Grades 3-5
Stack-n-Pack
Line Geometry ▪ Grades 3-5
Stack-n-Pack
Line Geometry ▪ Grades 3-5
Stack-n-Pack
Line Geometry ▪ Grades 3-5

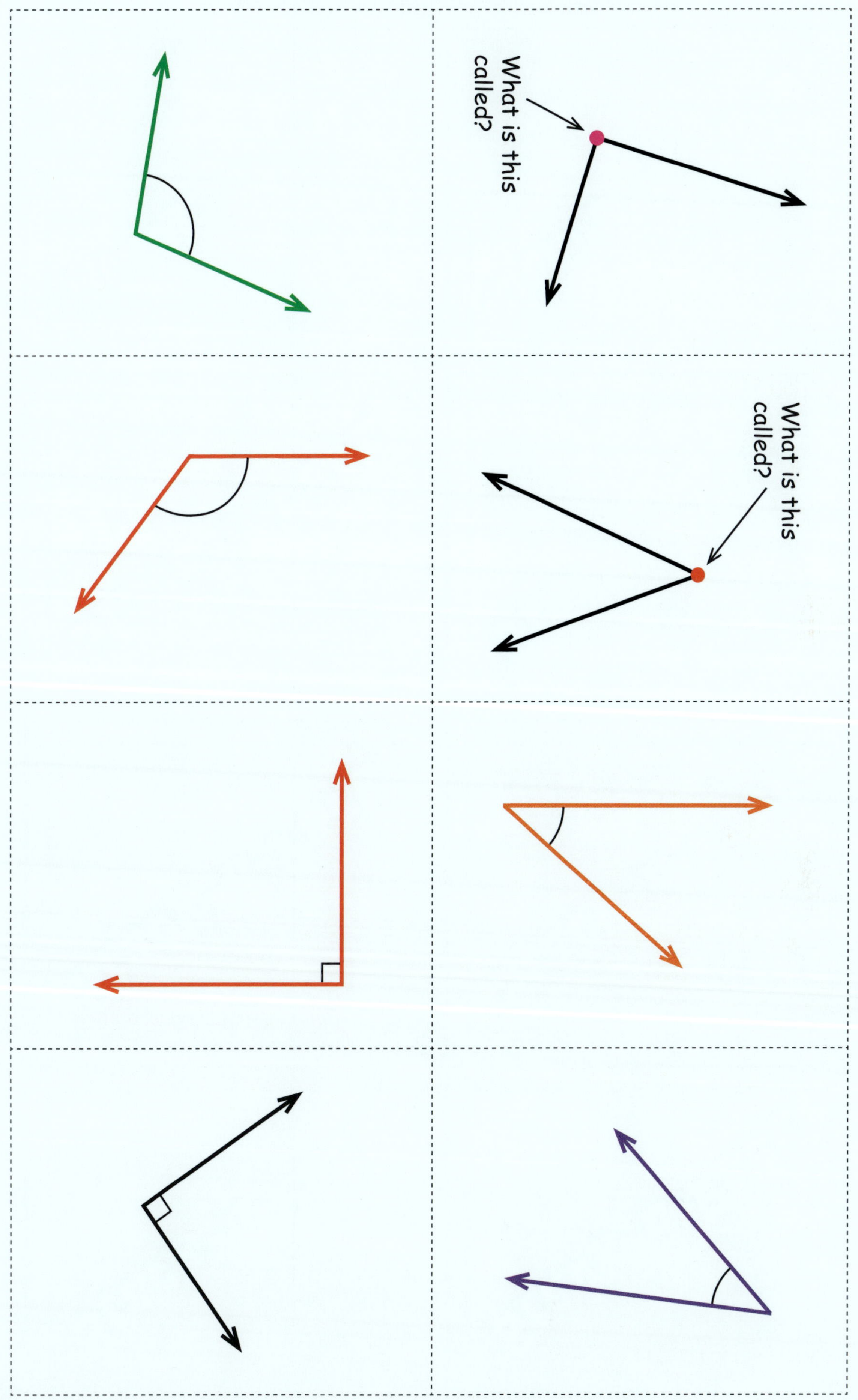
What is this called?
What is this called?

Stack-n-Pack
Line Geometry ▪ Grades 3-5
Stack-n-Pack
Line Geometry ▪ Grades 3-5
Stack-n-Pack
Line Geometry ▪ Grades 3-5
Stack-n-Pack
Line Geometry ▪ Grades 3-5
Stack-n-Pack
Line Geometry ▪ Grades 3-5
Stack-n-Pack
Line Geometry ▪ Grades 3-5
Stack-n-Pack
Line Geometry ▪ Grades 3-5
Stack-n-Pack
Line Geometry ▪ Grades 3-5

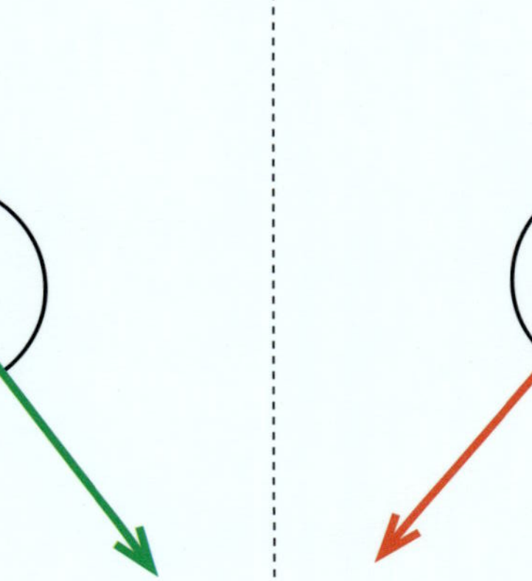

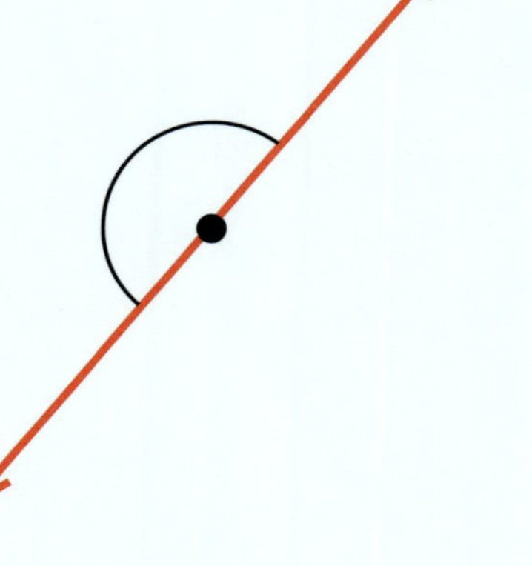

Lines in the same plane that never intersect.

Two lines that intersect at right angles.

Lines that have exactly one point in common.

An endless collection of points along a straight path with no endpoints.

A part of a line having two endpoints.

A part of a line that has one endpoint and goes on and on in one direction.

Stack-n-Pack
Line Geometry ▪ Grades 3-5

A line segment that passes through the center of a circle and has both endpoints on the circle.

A line segment with one endpoint on the circle and the other endpoint at the center.

A line segment with both endpoints on the circle.

The point of intersection of two rays when forming an angle.

An angle with a measure less than 90°.

An angle that measures 90°.

An angle with a measure greater than 90° but less than 180°.

An angle that measures 180°.

Stack-n-Pack
Line Geometry ▪ Grades 3-5
Stack-n-Pack
Line Geometry ▪ Grades 3-5
Stack-n-Pack
Line Geometry ▪ Grades 3-5
Stack-n-Pack
Line Geometry ▪ Grades 3-5
Stack-n-Pack
Line Geometry ▪ Grades 3-5
Stack-n-Pack
Line Geometry ▪ Grades 3-5
Stack-n-Pack
Line Geometry ▪ Grades 3-5
Stack-n-Pack
Line Geometry ▪ Grades 3-5

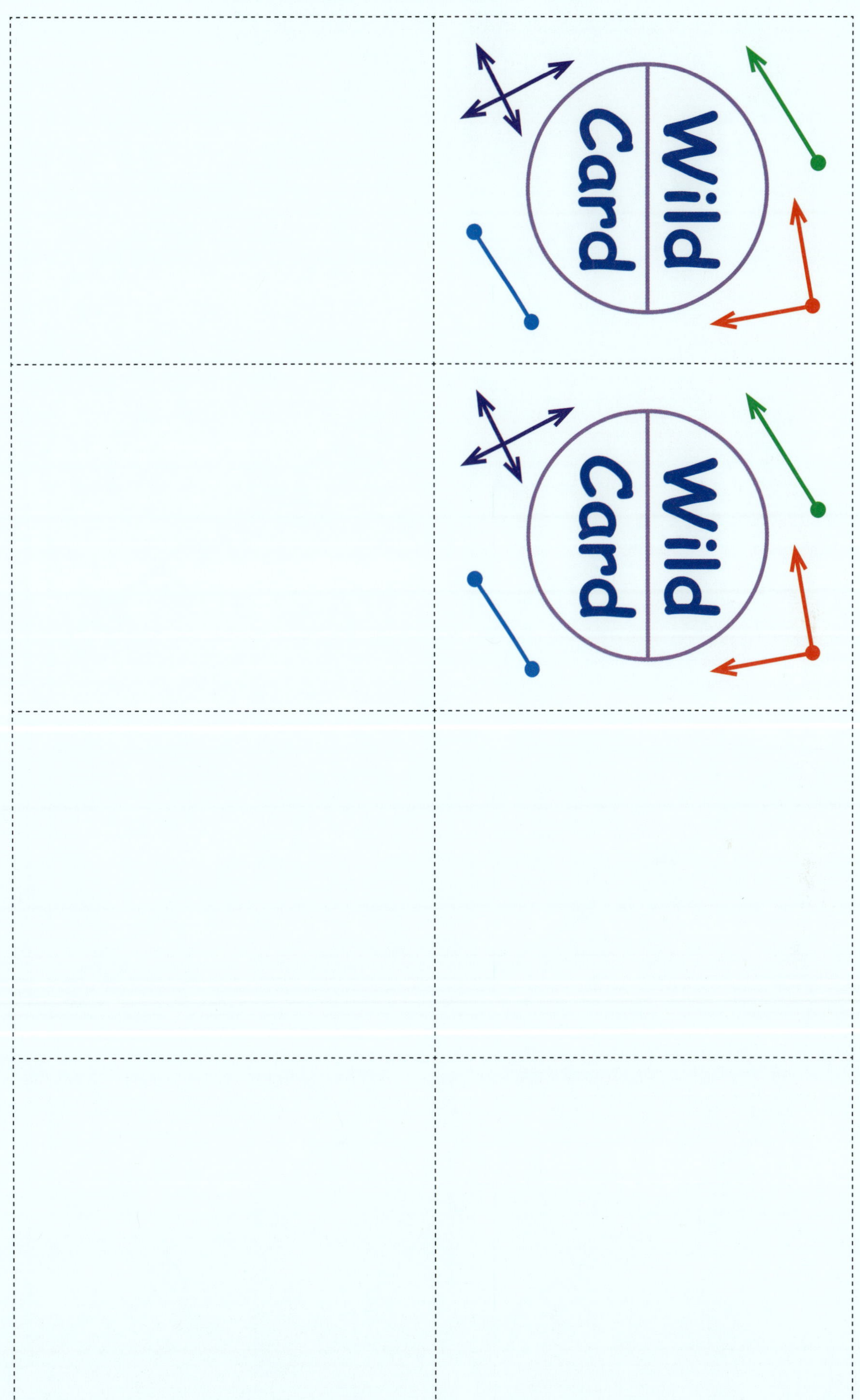
Wild
Card
Wild
Card

Stack-n-Pack
Line Geometry ▪ Grades 3-5
Stack-n-Pack
Line Geometry ▪ Grades 3-5
Stack-n-Pack
Line Geometry ▪ Grades 3-5
Stack-n-Pack
Line Geometry ▪ Grades 3-5
Stack-n-Pack
Line Geometry ▪ Grades 3-5
Stack-n-Pack
Line Geometry ▪ Grades 3-5
Stack-n-Pack
Line Geometry ▪ Grades 3-5
Stack-n-Pack
Line Geometry ▪ Grades 3-5

Area and Perimeter

Stack-n-Pack	Stack Starter	# of Cards in Completed Stack	Cards in the Completed Stack
Area and Perimeter	Shape (there are 2 of each shape)	4	Shape, Formulas, Area, Perimeter/ Circumference

Note: The Stack Starter is in blue.

Directions for Playing "Stack-n-Pack"

1. Form groups of 3-4 players.
2. Each player is dealt 4 cards. The remaining cards are placed face down in the center of the table. This is the draw pile. There is no discard pile.
3. Play begins with the person to the left of the dealer and continues clockwise around the table.
4. The first player can start a stack with the appropriate stack starter card (see Stack-n-Pack Information Chart above). This is NOT his/her stack. Any player can play on any stack. Once a stack has been started, the other cards in the stack may be played in any order. After playing his/her card, the first player draws a card from the draw pile ending his/her turn. If the first player does not have a stack starter, then he/she must PASS.

(Directions continued on back)

5. The next player has the option of playing on any stack laid on the table or beginning a new stack. Only ONE (1) card can be played at each turn. After playing his/her card, the player draws a card from the draw pile ending his/her turn.

6. Play continues in this manner with each player either playing on a stack or beginning a new one. Players must play if they are able. Otherwise, they must pass and lose their turn. Players must also remember to draw after they play their card.

7. A completed stack contains the total number of cards and representations described in the Stack-n-Pack Information Chart. The number of cards and representations necessary to complete a stack varies with each game. The player who completes the stack by playing the final card wins that stack.

8. Once all the cards have been drawn, play continues until no more cards can be played.

9. The game is over when the last stack has been completed. The player with the most stacks is the winner.

5 cm	$A = \pi r^2$ $C = \pi d$	A = 78.5 cm^2	C = 31.4 cm
5 cm	$A = b \times h$ $P = 4s$	A = 25 cm^2	P = 20 cm

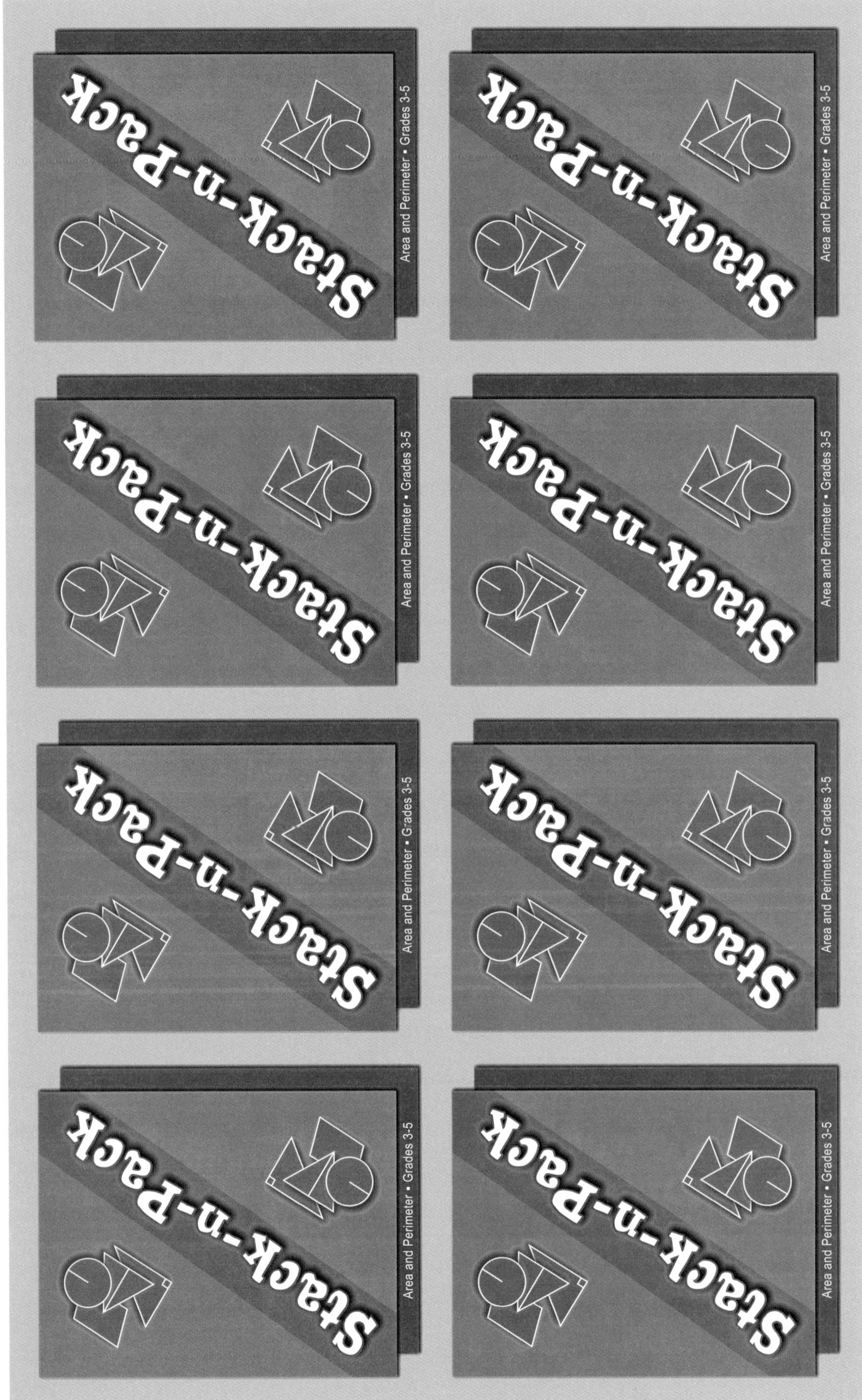
Stack-n-Pack
Area and Perimeter ▪ Grades 3-5
Stack-n-Pack
Area and Perimeter ▪ Grades 3-5
Stack-n-Pack
Area and Perimeter ▪ Grades 3-5
Stack-n-Pack
Area and Perimeter ▪ Grades 3-5
Stack-n-Pack
Area and Perimeter ▪ Grades 3-5
Stack-n-Pack
Area and Perimeter ▪ Grades 3-5
Stack-n-Pack
Area and Perimeter ▪ Grades 3-5
Stack-n-Pack
Area and Perimeter ▪ Grades 3-5

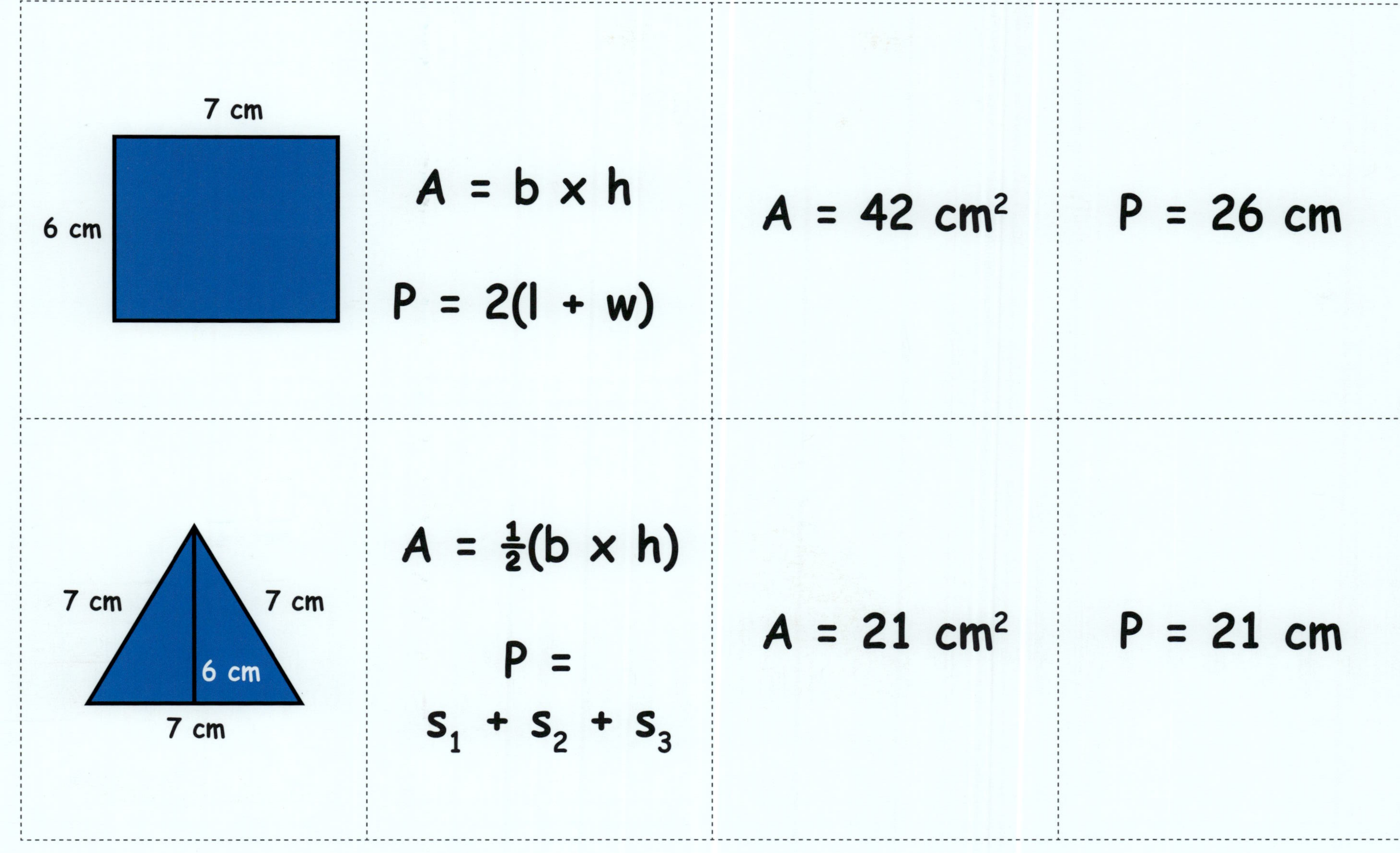
7 cm
6 cm
A = b × h
P = 2(l + w)
A = 42 cm²
P = 26 cm
7 cm
7 cm
6 cm
7 cm
A = ½(b × h)
P =
S1 + S2 + S3
A = 21 cm²
P = 21 cm

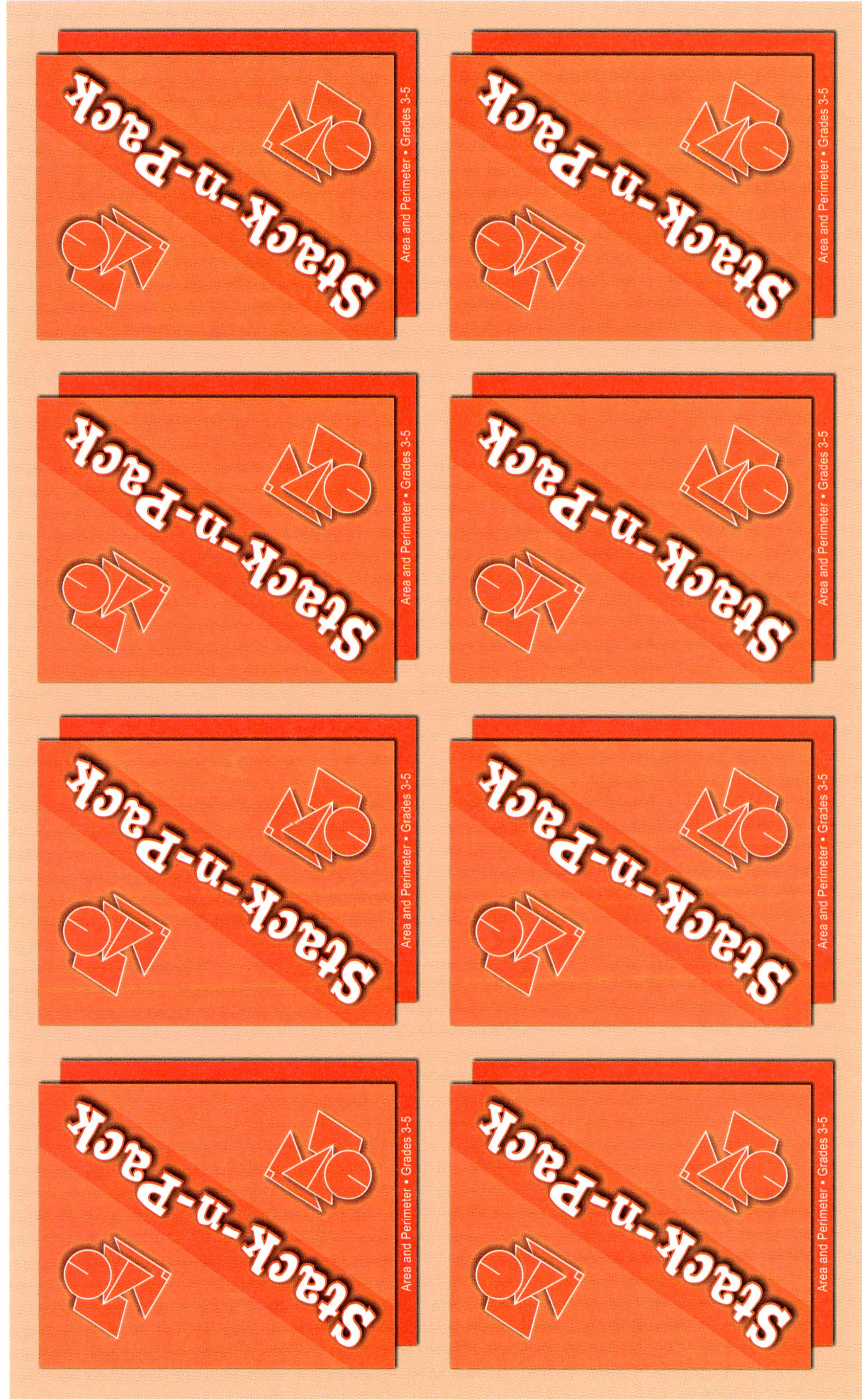
Stack-n-Pack
Area and Perimeter • Grades 3-5
Stack-n-Pack
Area and Perimeter • Grades 3-5
Stack-n-Pack
Area and Perimeter • Grades 3-5
Stack-n-Pack
Area and Perimeter • Grades 3-5
Stack-n-Pack
Area and Perimeter • Grades 3-5
Stack-n-Pack
Area and Perimeter • Grades 3-5
Stack-n-Pack
Area and Perimeter • Grades 3-5
Stack-n-Pack
Area and Perimeter • Grades 3-5

5 cm 4 cm 6 cm	$A = b \times h$ $P =$ $s_1 + s_2 + s_3 + s_4$	$A = 24\ cm^2$	$P = 22\ cm$
12 cm	$A = \pi r^2$ $C = \pi d$	$A =$ $113.04\ cm^2$	$C =$ $37.68\ cm$

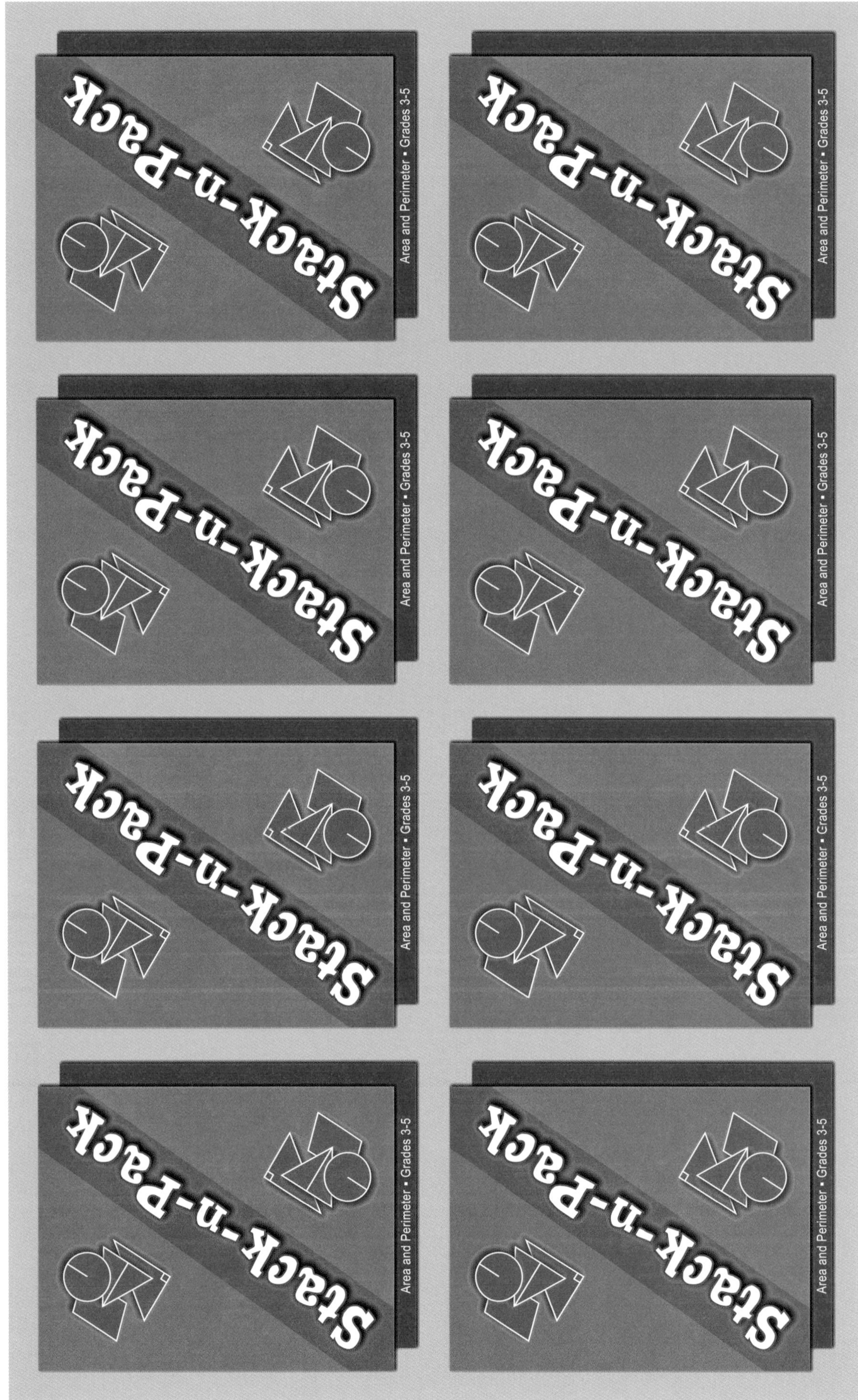
Stack-n-Pack
Area and Perimeter ▪ Grades 3-5
Stack-n-Pack
Area and Perimeter ▪ Grades 3-5
Stack-n-Pack
Area and Perimeter ▪ Grades 3-5
Stack-n-Pack
Area and Perimeter ▪ Grades 3-5
Stack-n-Pack
Area and Perimeter ▪ Grades 3-5
Stack-n-Pack
Area and Perimeter ▪ Grades 3-5
Stack-n-Pack
Area and Perimeter ▪ Grades 3-5
Stack-n-Pack
Area and Perimeter ▪ Grades 3-5

12 cm

5 cm

$A = b \times h$

$P = 2(l + w)$

$A = 60\ cm^2$

$P = 34\ cm$

8 cm

$A = b \times h$

$P = 4s$

$A = 64\ cm^2$

$P = 32\ cm$

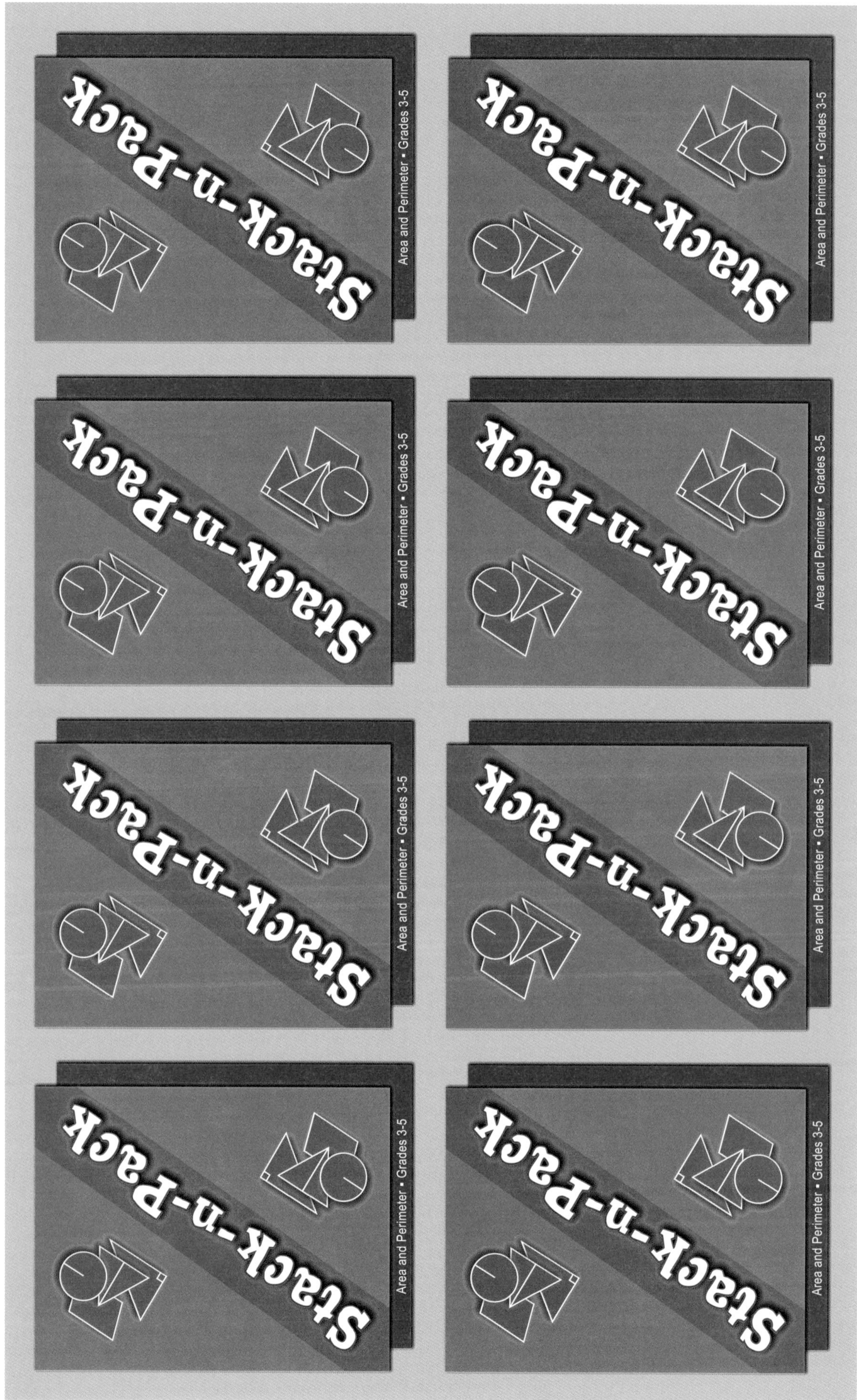
Stack-n-Pack
Area and Perimeter ▪ Grades 3-5

6 cm
10 cm
8 cm

$A = \frac{1}{2}(b \times h)$

$P =$

$s_1 + s_2 + s_3$

$A = 24\ cm^2$

$P = 24\ cm$

7 cm
8 cm
6 cm

$A = b \times h$

$P =$

$s_1 + s_2 + s_3 + s_4$

$A = 42\ cm^2$

$P = 28\ cm$

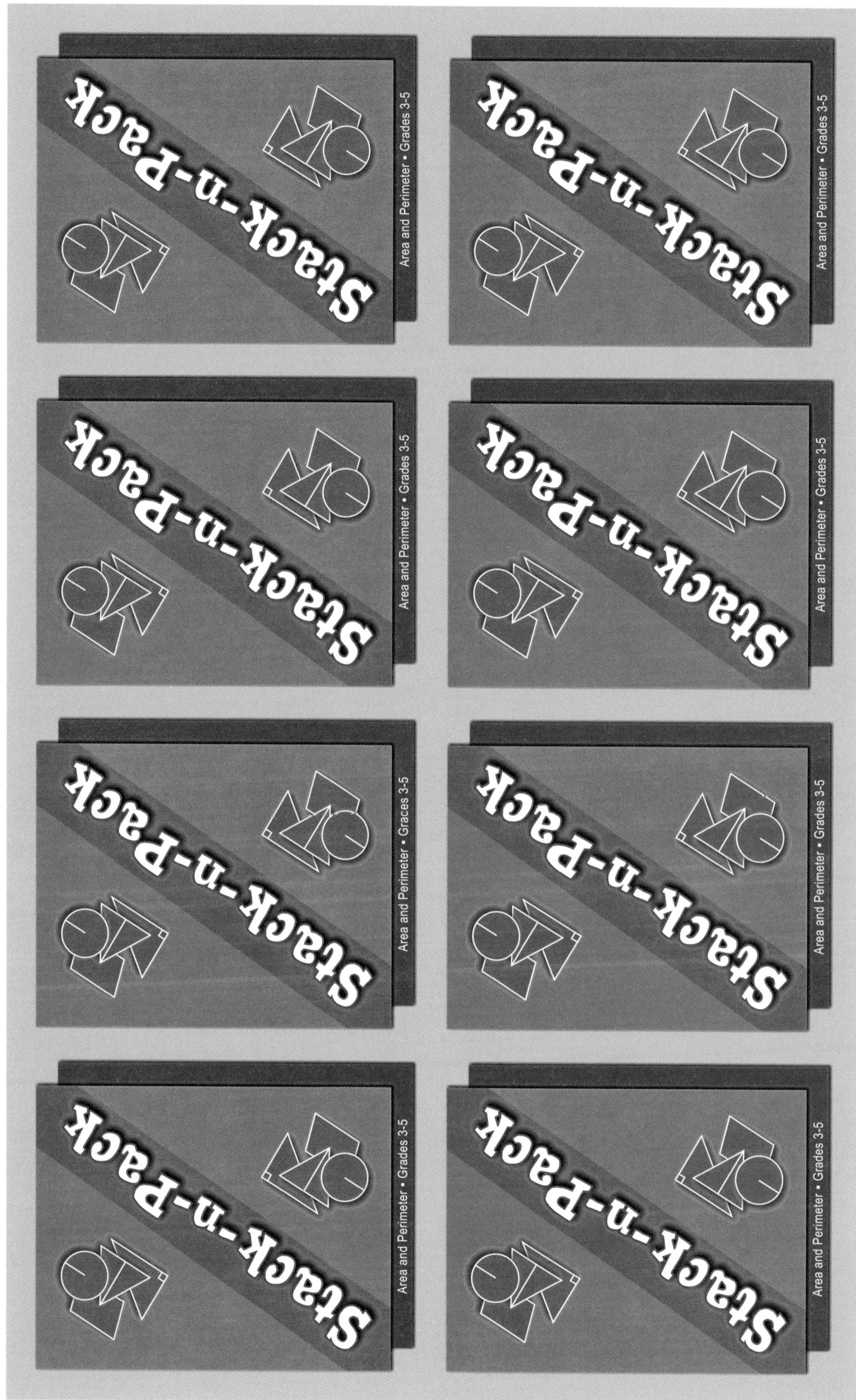
Stack-n-Pack
Area and Perimeter ▪ Grades 3-5
Stack-n-Pack
Area and Perimeter ▪ Grades 3-5
Stack-n-Pack
Area and Perimeter ▪ Grades 3-5
Stack-n-Pack
Area and Perimeter ▪ Grades 3-5
Stack-n-Pack
Area and Perimeter ▪ Graces 3-5
Stack-n-Pack
Area and Perimeter ▪ Grades 3-5
Stack-n-Pack
Area and Perimeter ▪ Grades 3-5
Stack-n-Pack
Area and Perimeter ▪ Grades 3-5

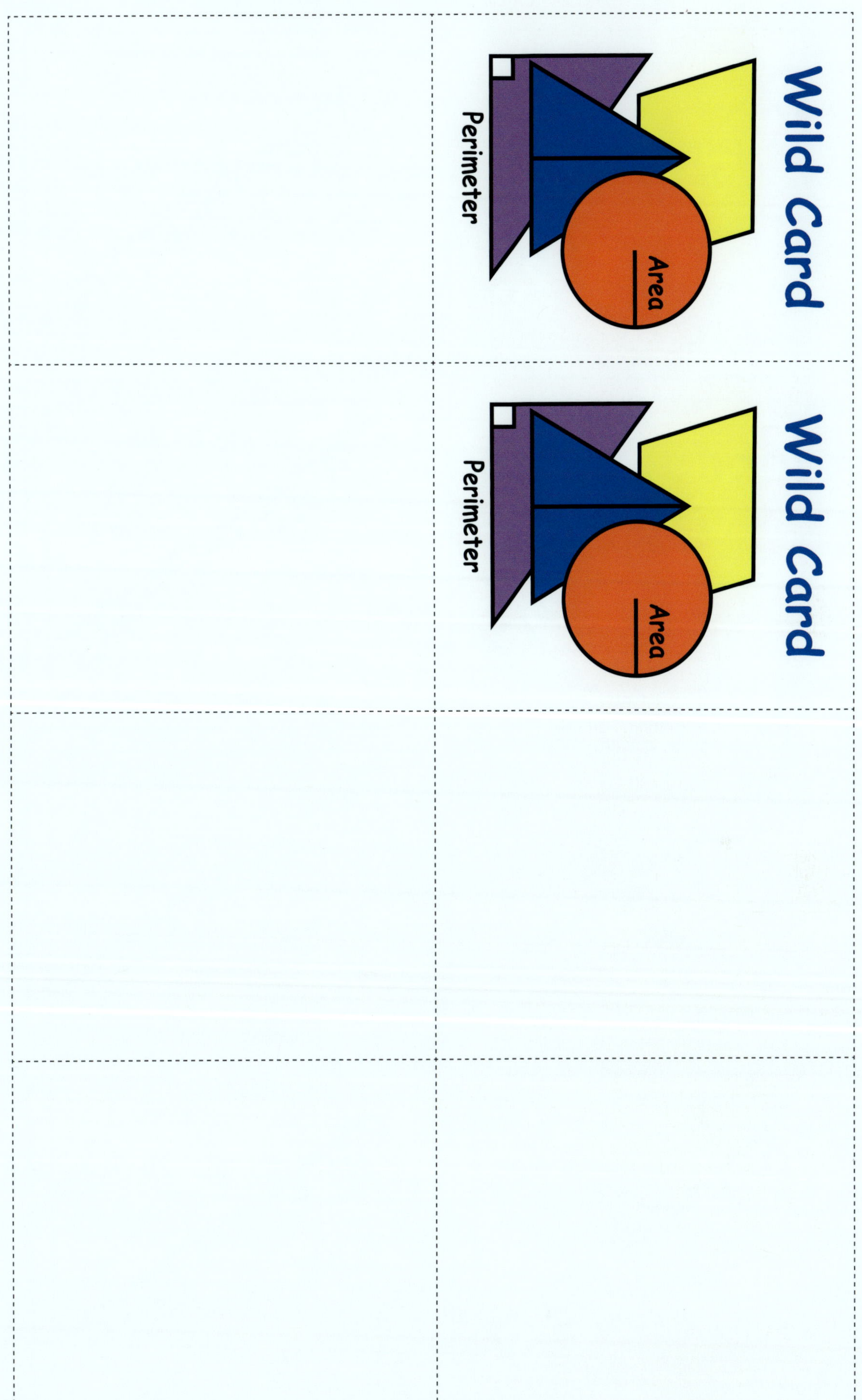
Wild Card
Perimeter
Area
Wild Card
Perimeter
Area

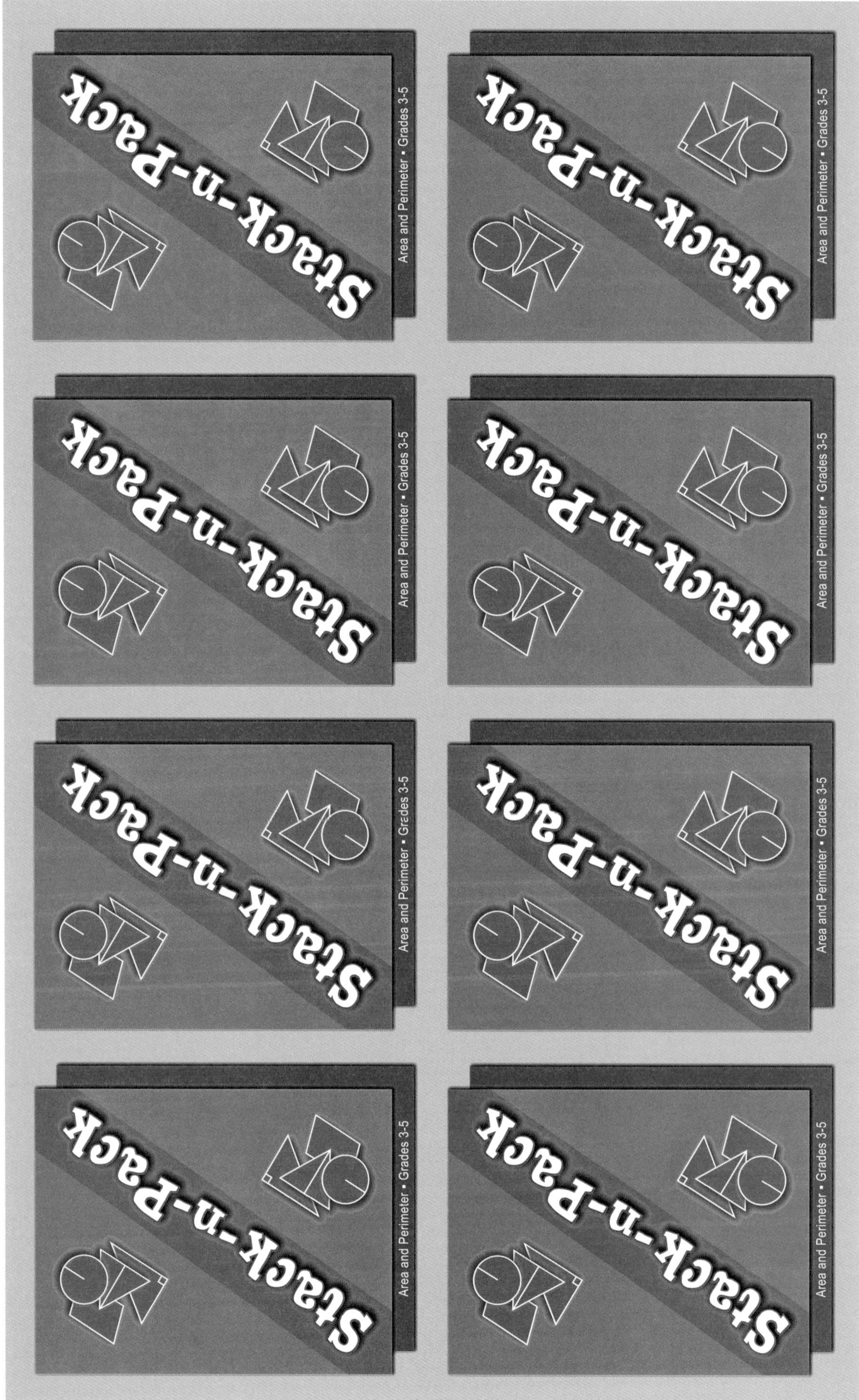
Stack-n-Pack
Area and Perimeter ▪ Grades 3-5

Algebraic Reasoning

Stack-n-Pack	Stack Starter	# of Cards in Completed Stack	Cards in the Completed Stack
Algebraic Reasoning	Variable with Answer (☆=4)	3	Variable, 2 Equations That Have the Same Value as the Variable

Note: The Stack Starter is in blue.

Directions for Playing "Stack-n-Pack"

1. Form groups of 3-4 players.
2. Each player is dealt 4 cards. The remaining cards are placed face down in the center of the table. This is the draw pile. There is no discard pile.
3. Play begins with the person to the left of the dealer and continues clockwise around the table.
4. The first player can start a stack with the appropriate stack starter card (see Stack-n-Pack Information Chart above). This is NOT his/her stack. Any player can play on any stack. Once a stack has been started, the other cards in the stack may be played in any order. After playing his/her card, the first player draws a card from the draw pile ending his/her turn. If the first player does not have a stack starter, then he/she must PASS.

(Directions continued on back)

5. The next player has the option of playing on any stack laid on the table or beginning a new stack. Only ONE (1) card can be played at each turn. After playing his/her card, the player draws a card from the draw pile ending his/her turn.

6. Play continues in this manner with each player either playing on a stack or beginning a new one. Players must play if they are able. Otherwise, they must pass and lose their turn. Players must also remember to draw after they play their card.

7. A completed stack contains the total number of cards and representations described in the Stack-n-Pack Information Chart. The number of cards and representations necessary to complete a stack varies with each game. The player who completes the stack by playing the final card wins that stack.

8. Once all the cards have been drawn, play continues until no more cards can be played.

9. The game is over when the last stack has been completed. The player with the most stacks is the winner.

$\triangle \times 6 = 12$	☆ = 4
$10 \div 5 = \triangle$	$3 \times$ ☆ $= 12$
◇ = 45	☆ $- 1 = 3$
$9 \times 5 =$ ◇	$\triangle = 2$

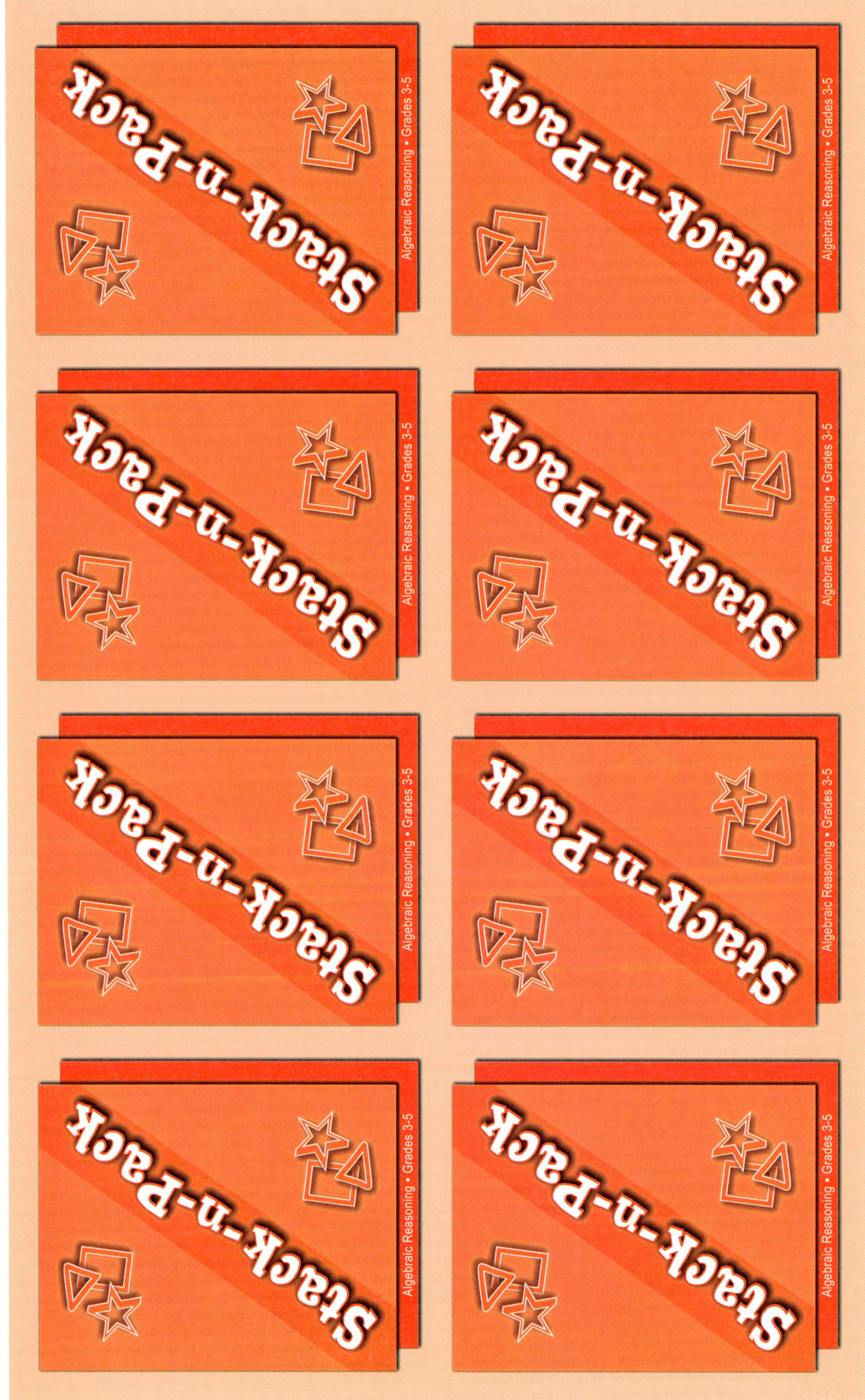
Stack-n-Pack
Algebraic Reasoning • Grades 3-5
Stack-n-Pack
Algebraic Reasoning • Grades 3-5
Stack-n-Pack
Algebraic Reasoning • Grades 3-5
Stack-n-Pack
Algebraic Reasoning • Grades 3-5
Stack-n-Pack
Algebraic Reasoning • Grades 3-5
Stack-n-Pack
Algebraic Reasoning • Grades 3-5
Stack-n-Pack
Algebraic Reasoning • Grades 3-5
Stack-n-Pack
Algebraic Reasoning • Grades 3-5

□ = 25

◇ - 28 = 17

125 ÷ 5 = □

□ = 8

76 - □ = 51

□ × 6 = 48

☆ = 15

15 - □ = 7

Stack-n-Pack
Algebraic Reasoning ▪ Grades 3-5
Stack-n-Pack
Algebraic Reasoning ▪ Grades 3-5
Stack-n-Pack
Algebraic Reasoning ▪ Grades 3-5
Stack-n-Pack
Algebraic Reasoning ▪ Grades 3-5
Stack-n-Pack
Algebraic Reasoning ▪ Grades 3-5
Stack-n-Pack
Algebraic Reasoning ▪ Grades 3-5
Stack-n-Pack
Algebraic Reasoning ▪ Grades 3-5
Stack-n-Pack
Algebraic Reasoning ▪ Grades 3-5

$72 \div 6 = \triangle$	$☆ \div 5 = 3$
$\diamond = 7$	$☆ + 17 = 32$
$\diamond \times 8 = 56$	$\triangle = 12$
$63 \div \diamond = 9$	$\triangle \times 3 = 36$

Stack-n-Pack
Algebraic Reasoning ▪ Grades 3-5
Stack-n-Pack
Algebraic Reasoning ▪ Grades 3-5
Stack-n-Pack
Algebraic Reasoning ▪ Grades 3-5
Stack-n-Pack
Algebraic Reasoning ▪ Grades 3-5
Stack-n-Pack
Algebraic Reasoning ▪ Grades 3-5
Stack-n-Pack
Algebraic Reasoning ▪ Grades 3-5
Stack-n-Pack
Algebraic Reasoning ▪ Grades 3-5
Stack-n-Pack
Algebraic Reasoning ▪ Grades 3-5

54 ÷ 6 = □	☆ = 32
□ × 3 = 27	☆ ÷ 4 = 8
◇ = 75	54 - ☆ = 22
45 + 30 = ◇	9 = □

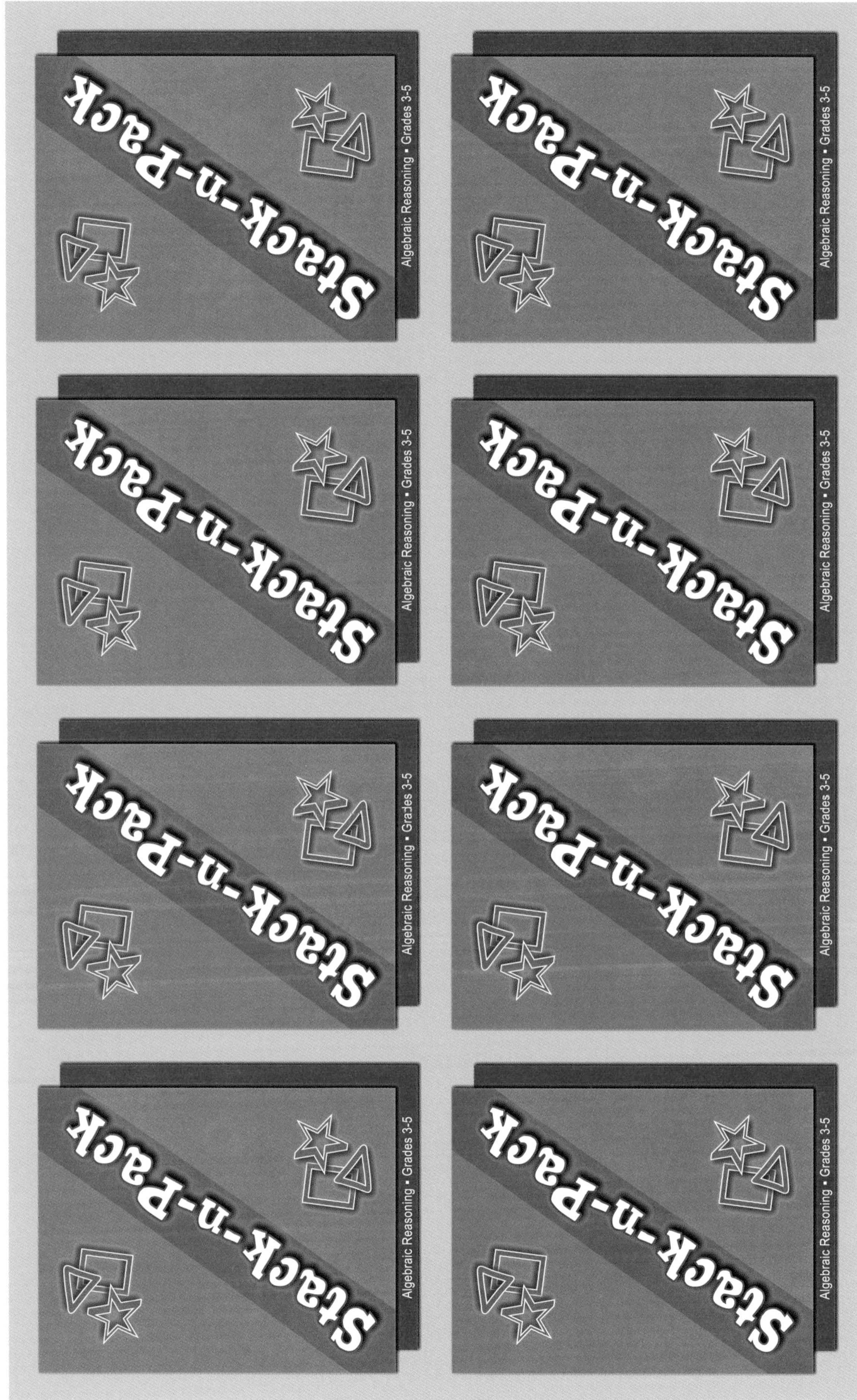
Stack-n-Pack
Algebraic Reasoning ▪ Grades 3-5
Stack-n-Pack
Algebraic Reasoning ▪ Grades 3-5
Stack-n-Pack
Algebraic Reasoning ▪ Grades 3-5
Stack-n-Pack
Algebraic Reasoning ▪ Grades 3-5
Stack-n-Pack
Algebraic Reasoning ▪ Grades 3-5
Stack-n-Pack
Algebraic Reasoning ▪ Grades 3-5
Stack-n-Pack
Algebraic Reasoning ▪ Grades 3-5
Stack-n-Pack
Algebraic Reasoning ▪ Grades 3-5

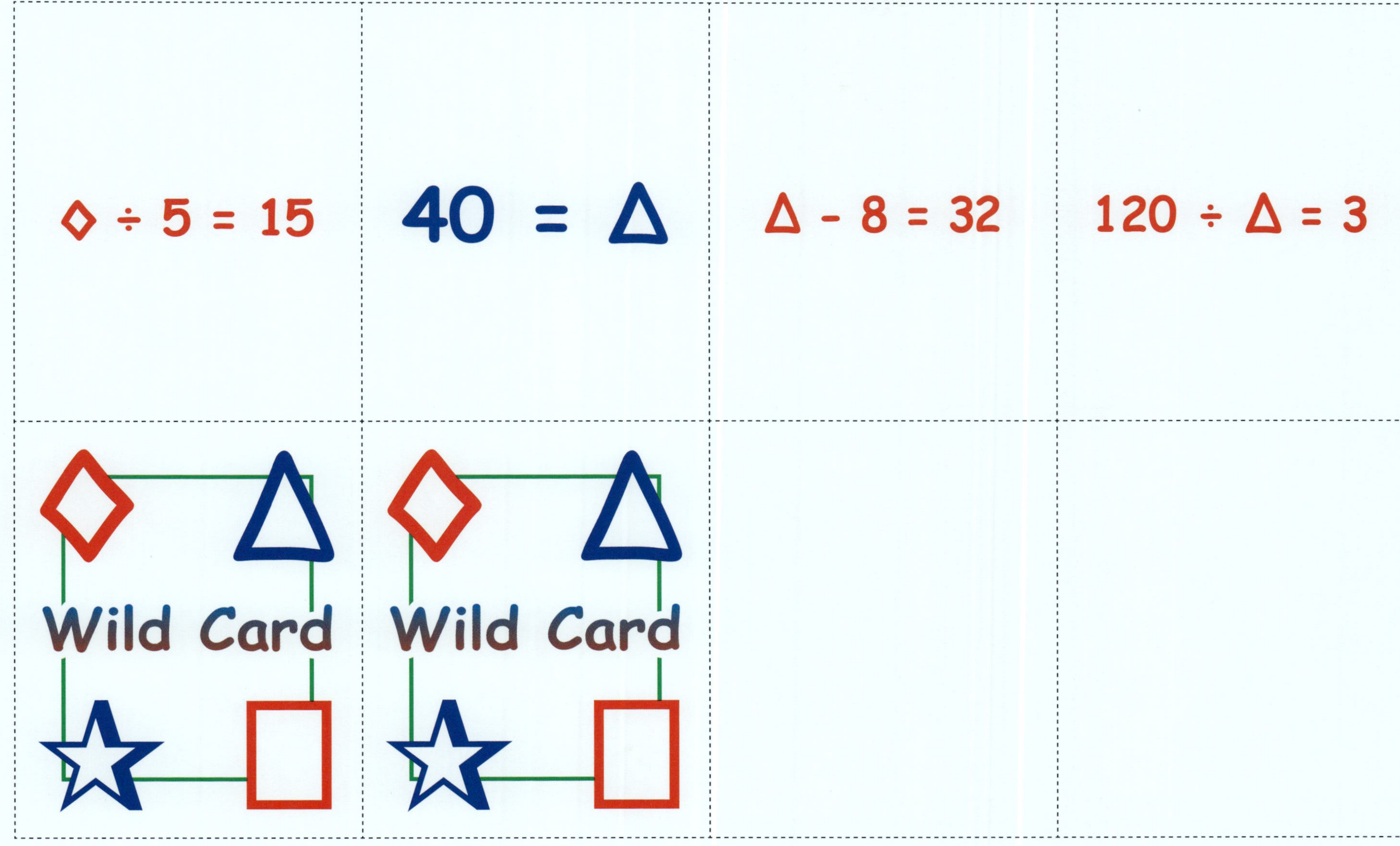
◇ ÷ 5 = 15
40 = △
△ - 8 = 32
120 ÷ △ = 3
Wild Card
Wild Card

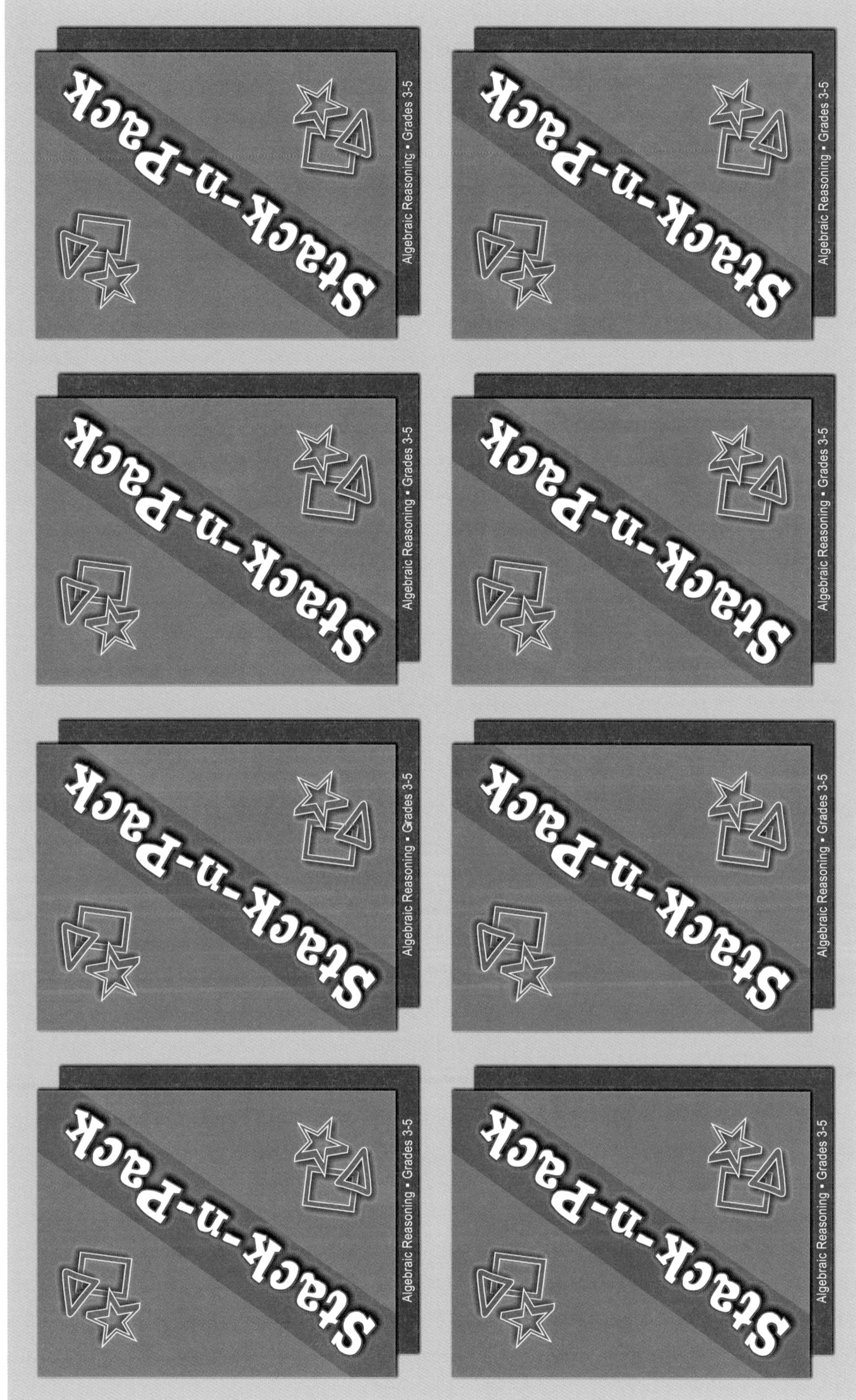
Stack-n-Pack
Algebraic Reasoning ▪ Grades 3-5
Stack-n-Pack
Algebraic Reasoning ▪ Grades 3-5
Stack-n-Pack
Algebraic Reasoning ▪ Grades 3-5
Stack-n-Pack
Algebraic Reasoning ▪ Grades 3-5
Stack-n-Pack
Algebraic Reasoning ▪ Grades 3-5
Stack-n-Pack
Algebraic Reasoning ▪ Grades 3-5
Stack-n-Pack
Algebraic Reasoning ▪ Grades 3-5
Stack-n-Pack
Algebraic Reasoning ▪ Grades 3-5

Answer Key

Place Value Identification

1. ones; $13,45\underline{6}$; $36\underline{2}$; $42\underline{1}.23$
2. tens; $5\underline{3}9$; $1,3\underline{5}2$; $1,2\underline{8}9.251$;
3. hundreds; $\underline{7}49$; $23,\underline{8}99$; $15,\underline{6}32.4$
4. thousands; $\underline{3},002$; $11\underline{5},341$; $28\underline{9},333$
5. ten thousands; $\underline{6}8,219.3$; $3\underline{8}9,214$; $1\underline{2}7,451$
6. hundred thousands; $\underline{2}90,571.23$; $\underline{5}00,000$; $1,\underline{3}45,890$
7. millions; $4\underline{5},689,123$; $1\underline{6},234,589$; $\underline{9},123,490.1$
8. tenths; $75.\underline{8}$; $5,321.\underline{2}34$; $438.\underline{9}4$
9. hundredths; $1,257.3\underline{4}1$; $732.5\underline{0}9$; $0.5\underline{6}1$
10. thousandths; $2.65\underline{1}1$; $148.93\underline{2}$; $0.29\underline{7}21$
11. ten-thousandths; $61.298\underline{1}$; $0.973\underline{4}1$; $267.213\underline{0}$

Multiplication Facts

1. 24; 6 • 4; 8 • 3; 12 • 2
2. 12; 3 • 4; 6 • 2; 12 • 1
3. 36; 6 • 6; 12 • 3; 9 • 4
4. 30; 5 • 6; 3 • 10; 15 • 2
5. 18; 3 • 6; 9 • 2; 6 • 3
6. 48; 6 • 8; 4 • 12; 24 • 2
7. 20; 5 • 4; 2 • 10; 4 • 5
8. 40; 5 • 8; 4 • 10; 8 • 5
9. 45; 9 • 5; 15 • 3; 5 • 9
10. 60; 12 • 5; 15 • 4; 6 • 10
11. 32; 4 • 8; 16 • 2; 8 • 4

2-D and 3-D Geometric Shapes

1. Rectangle; 
2. Circle; 
3. Triangle; 
4. Square; 
5. Rhombus; 
6. Ellipse; 
7. Pentagon; 
8. Hexagon; 
9. Octagon;   
10. Parallelogram; 
11. Rectangular Prism; 
12. Cylinder; 
13. Cube;
14. Cone;

Polygon Classification

1. Equilateral Triangle; red triangle; This triangle has all 3 sides congruent; This triangle has all 3 angles are 60°
2. Isosceles Triangle; yellow triangle; This triangle has 2 or more congruent sides; This triangle has at least 2 angles with the same degree
3. Scalene Triangle, white triangle; This triangle has no congruent sides; This triangle has no congruent angles
4. Square; green square; This parallelogram has 4 congruent sides; this parallelogram has 4 right angles
5. Rectangle; orange rectangle; This parallelogram has 4 sides, but they are not all congruent; This parallelogram has 4 right angles
6. Parallelogram; green parallelogram; This quadrilateral has 2 pairs of parallel sides; This quadrilateral has 2 obtuse and 2 acute angles
7. Rhombus; purple rhombus; This parallelogram has 4 congruent sides; This parallelogram has 2 pairs of congruent angles
8. Trapezoid; yellow trapezoid; This quadrilateral has exactly one pair of parallel sides; This quadrilateral's angles vary with the lengths of the side
9. Regular Pentagon; orange pentagon; This polygon has 5 congruent sides; Each interior angle of this polygon measures 108°
10. Regular Hexagon; green hexagon; This polygon has 6 congruent sides; Each interior angle of this polygon measures 120°
11. Regular Octagon; orange octagon; This polygon has 8 congruent sides; Each interior angle of this polygon measures 135°

LCM and GCF

1. 6, 8; LCM = 24; GCF = 2
2. 3, 9; LCM = 9; GCF = 3
3. 4, 32; LCM = 32; GCF = 4
4. 5, 6; LCM = 30; GCF = 1
5. 10, 15; LCM = 30; GCF = 5
6. 8, 24; LCM = 24; GCF = 8
7. 6, 36; LCM = 36; GCF = 6
8. 14, 21; LCM = 42; GCF = 7
9. 20, 10, 60; LCM = 60; GCF = 10
10. 6, 15, 3; LCM = 30; GCF = 3
11. 16, 32, 4; LCM = 32; GCF = 4
12. 64, 32, 16; LCM = 64; GCF = 16
13. 2, 4, 11; LCM = 44; GCF = 1
14. 6, 4, 18; LCM = 36; GCF = 2
15. 3, 4, 6; LCM = 12; GCF = 1
16. 7, 21, 42; LCM = 42; GCF = 7

Equivalent Fractions

1. 1/2; 2/4;  ; 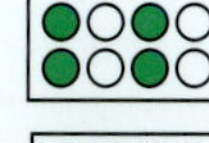
2. 1/3; 3/9; 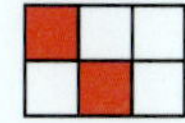 ; 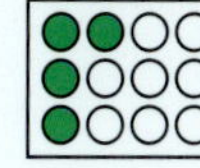

Answer Key

Equivalent Fractions (cont.)

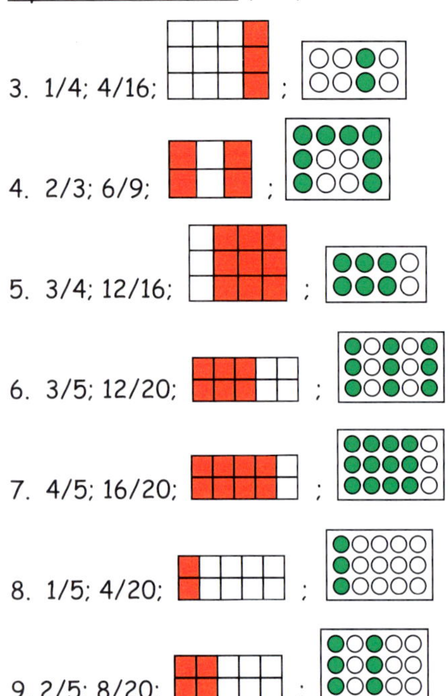

3. 1/4; 4/16; ;
4. 2/3; 6/9; ;
5. 3/4; 12/16; ;
6. 3/5; 12/20; ;
7. 4/5; 16/20; ;
8. 1/5; 4/20; ;
9. 2/5; 8/20; ;

Addition and Multiplication Properties

1. Commutative Property of Addition; a + b = b + a; 3 + 5 = 5 + 3; 43 + 95; 95 + 43
2. Associative Property of Addition; a + (b + c) = (a + b) + c; 3 + (2 + 6) = (3 + 2) + 6; 15 + (10 + 43) = (15 + 10) + 43
3. Additive Identity; a + 0 = a; 8 + 0 = 8; 33 + 0 = 33
4. Multiplicative Identity; a • 1 = a; 4 • 1 = 4; 65 • 1 = 65
5. Distributive Property; a(c + b) = ac + ab; 7(4 + 8) = 7(4) + 7(8); 41(2 + 25) = 41(2) + 41(25)
6. Associative Property of Multiplication; a • (b • c) = (a • b) • c; 7 • (2 • 5) = (7 • 2) • 5; 21 • (14 • 50) = (21 • 14) • 50
7. Commutative Property of Multiplication; a • b = b • a; 5 • 7 = 7 • 5; 22 • 18 = 18 • 22
8. Zero Product Property; a • b = 0, then a = 0 or b = 0; 5 • 0 = 0; 84 • 0 = 0

Line Geometry

1. Parallel Lines; 2 red parallel lines; 2 green parallel lines; Lines in the same plane that never intersect
2. Perpendicular Lines; 2 purple perpendicular lines; 2 black perpendicular lines; Two lines that intersect at right angles
3. Intersecting Lines; 2 red intersecting lines; 2 green intersecting lines; Lines that have exactly one point in common
4. Line; orange line; black line; An endless collection of points along a straight path with no endpoints
5. Line Segment; purple line segment; red line segment; A part of a line have two endpoints
6. Ray; purple ray; green ray; A part of a line that has one endpoint and goes on and on in one direction
7. Diameter; pink diameter; red diameter; A line segment that passes through the center of the circle and has both endpoints on the circle
8. Radius; orange radius; purple radius; A line segment with one endpoint on the circle and the other endpoint at the center
9. Chord; green chord; orange chord; A line segment with both endpoints on the circle (but not a diameter)
10. Vertex; pink vertex; red vertex; The point of intersection of two rays when forming an angle
11. Acute Angle; orange acute angle; purple acute angle; An angle with a measure less than 90°
12. Obtuse Angle; green obtuse angle; red obtuse angle; An angle with a measure greater than 90° but less than 180°
13. Right Angle; red right angle; black right angle; An angle that measures 90°
14. Straight Angle; green straight angle; red straight angle; An angle that measures 180°

Area and Perimeter

1. Dark Blue Circle; $A = \pi r^2$, $C = \pi d$; $A = 78.5\ cm^2$; $C = 31.4$ cm
2. Light Blue Circle; $A = \pi r^2$, $C = \pi d$; $A = 113.04\ cm^2$; $C = 37.68$ cm
3. Dark Blue Square; A = b x h, P = 4s; $A = 25\ cm^2$; P = 20 cm
4. Light Blue Square; A = b x h; P = 4s; $A = 64\ cm^2$; P = 32 cm
5. Dark Blue Rectangle; A = b x h, P = 2(l + w); A = $42\ cm^2$; P = 26 cm
6. Light Blue Rectangle; A = b x h, P = 2(l + w); A = $60\ cm^2$; P = 34 cm
7. Dark Blue Triangle; $A = \frac{1}{2}(b \times h)$, $P = s_1 + s_2 + s_3$; $A = 21\ cm^2$; P = 21 cm
8. Light Blue Triangle; $A = \frac{1}{2}(b \times h)$, $P = s_1 + s_2 + s_3$; $A = 24\ cm^2$; P = 24 cm
9. Dark Blue Parallelogram; A = b x h, $P = s_1 + s_2 + s_3 + s_4$; $A = 24\ cm^2$; P = 22 cm
10. Light Blue Parallelogram; A = b x h, $P = s_1 + s_2 + s_3 + s_4$; $A = 42\ cm^2$; P = 28 cm

Algebraic Reasoning

1. ☆ = 4; 3 x ☆ = 12; ☆ - 1 = 3
2. △ = 2; △ x 6 = 12; 10 ÷ 5 = △
3. ◇ = 45; 9 x 5 = ◇; ◇ - 28 = 17
4. □ = 8; □ x 6 = 48; 15 - □ = 7
5. □ = 25; 125 ÷ 5 = □; 76 - □ = 51
6. ☆ = 15; ☆ ÷ 5 = 3; ☆ + 17 = 32
7. △ = 12; △ x 3 = 36; 72 ÷ 6 = △
8. ◇ = 7; ◇ x 8 = 56; 63 ÷ 9 = ◇
9. ☆ = 32; ☆ ÷ 4 = 8; 54 - ☆ = 22
10. 9 = □ ; 54 ÷ 6 = □; □ x 3 = 27
11. ◇ = 75; 45 + 30 = ◇; ◇ ÷ 5 = 15
12. 40 = △; △ - 8 = 32; 120 ÷ △ = 3